MW00474324

TRUCKEROLOGY

Have a Great Day! ☺
Long Haul

Have a Great Day! :)
Long Hou!

TRUCKEROLOGY

MOVING STORIES FROM AN AMERICAN TRUCKER

LONG-HAUL LARRY

ePublishingWorks!
love what you read.

Without limiting the rights under copyright(s) reserved below, no part of this publication may be reproduced, stored in or introduced into a retrieval system, or transmitted, in any form, or by any means (electronic, mechanical, photocopying, recording, or otherwise) without the prior permission of the publisher and the copyright owner.

This work is intended for entertainment purposes only.

The scanning, uploading, and distributing of this book via the internet or via any other means without the permission of the publisher and copyright owner is illegal and punishable by law. Please purchase only authorized copies, and do not participate in or encourage piracy of copyrighted materials. Your support of the author's rights is appreciated.

Copyright © 2020 by ePublishing Works!. All rights reserved.

Photography by: Brian W. Paules

Book and cover design by eBook Prep
www.ebookprep.com

June, 2020
ISBN: 978-1-64457-157-6

ePublishing Works!
644 Shrewsbury Commons Ave
Ste 249
Shrewsbury PA 17361
United States of America

www.epublishingworks.com
Phone: 866-846-5123

CONTENTS

To my loyal YouTube subscribers, and John at JBG Travels, without whom this would never have been possible. Thank you!

"...It is only the Lord's mercies that have kept us from complete destruction. Great is his faithfulness; his loving-kindness begins afresh each day."

— LAMENTATIONS 3:22-23

INTRODUCTION

BY JOHN VOLLRATH, JBG TRAVELS

Larry and I bonded over an obsession. It was supposed to be a hobby but it really was an obsession.

Larry used to co-own and manage a hobby store called Hobbytown USA near Sheboygan, Wisconsin.

It was around 1998, I was a twenty-three-year-old on-and-off-again truck driver, living in my dad's basement and heavily consumed with building radio-controlled airplanes. I bought a lot of stuff from Larry's store. That's how we met.

We also both belonged to a local radio-controlled airplane club where we were the oddballs. Everyone in the club was really uptight about not crashing their planes. Larry and I would spend our flying time trying to hit each other in the air.

I guess you could say we became friends over a shared obsession and a mutual desire for destruction.

Larry and I would fly anything. If it had wings—or something that looked like wings—we'd put an engine and a propeller on it and make it fly. It was a lot of fun for many years.

Larry's the kind of guy who's always thinking, can turn anything into fun, and knows how to make things happen. He may also have a squirrel cage in his head, one that's always spinning out new ideas.

In our town of Sheboygan, there wasn't much for people to do. But we had lots of lakes and rivers. So Larry got the idea of selling radio-controlled boats, and soon the Kiwanis park was full of people racing boats on the Sheboygan River.

It was fun for lots of people and Larry made it happen. He saw a need and created a solution. That's the kind of guy he is.

Of course, somebody had to come along and complain to the "town fathers" which pretty much put an end to it. But it sure was fun while it lasted!

Larry's also the kind of guy who knows when to show up.

We each rented a storage unit across from where I was living with my dad. That's where we did our hobby work.

One Saturday morning I got up, planning to head over to my unit, and discovered my dad had died in his sleep, sometime during the night. The medics said around 2 AM. The first person I told was Larry.

Next thing I knew, Larry, who was across the street, was at the door. He walked in and gave me a big hug.

You gotta know that Larry's not a guy who expresses his feelings much—he's a manly, man. But that day I needed a hug and it came from an unlikely place. I'll never forget it.

After my dad passed—that was around 2001—I had to get serious about working. It was just me, now, no dad to mooch on, so I got more serious about my truck driving career.

Which brings me back to Larry.

Larry's a quick learner and largely self-taught.

One evening I asked Larry to go on a night run with me from Wisconsin to somewhere around Philadelphia, Pennsylvania.

Larry agreed, hopped in the passenger seat and off we went in my 10 speed truck.

He seemed interested in the mechanics of shifting so I told him to put his hand on the gear shift and not to move a muscle, just feel the gears. Then, without making a big deal of it, I put my hand over his and let him feel the gears mesh as I did the shifting. This is the first and last time I held hands with Long-Haul Larry...we both pretended it wasn't awkward.

With Larry feeling the gears and watching my feet and movements, he learned how to drive a 10 speed transmission in about five or ten minutes.

Now, I do hesitate to confess to this next part, but I set the cruise control, we traded places, and Larry immediately became a truck driver as he drove from Port Washington to Wisconsin.

I've never known anyone to pick up something so complex so quickly, even though he'd grind a gear from time to time.

When we hit the Illinois state line, I took over before the toll roads. Switching seats, I noticed Larry looked kind of pale, like he'd seen a ghost. So I asked him, "how was it?"

He said, "*That* was really something!"

I could tell the trucking bug had bitten.

Afterward, he went to a professional truck driving school, and that's how Long-Haul Larry was born.

But Larry is so much more than a quick learner who knows how to make things fun, a faithful friend who knows when to show up, and a good truck driver who also knows how to fix 'em. He's also a gifted storyteller.

And, no matter how much this may surprise you or me, there is no one more surprised than Larry's high-school English teacher who often banished Larry to the hallway for one squirrel-brained prank or another.

To her I say, "Look at what Larry did, now!"

Ain't I a stinka'?

So it's my honor to introduce you to my long-time friend, truck driver, mechanic, and now storyteller extraordinaire, Long-Haul Larry.

Peace.

John Vollrath

JBG Travels

HOW IT ALL BEGAN

I was about 14 years old, growing up on the farm when my father came back from being in the hospital for about a year. He'd broken his neck and was paralyzed through much of his hospital stay. When he was able to walk again, he returned to the farm but wasn't able to continue farming.

So, my older brothers started venturing off into different jobs. Two of them started driving semis.

My next older brother, who is four years older than me, started hauling steel for a local company. He got paid by the pound, so the more weight he hauled, the more he got paid.

He'd pick up a load in Gary, Indiana, then he would go up to Green Bay, Wisconsin and even farther north.

Along the way, he'd come by the house and pick me up. He was always really tired, so as soon as we went on the road, he'd put the cruise control on, jump out of the seat and I would jump in and drive up the highways. Then he'd crawl in the back for a little bit of sleep.

That's how I got a taste for driving a truck.

Another one of my brothers drove for several years until he was in a mega accident. He was heading southbound on a highway when a lady fell asleep, crossed the median, and went right up underneath his trailer. It was not pretty.

She ended up dying and my brother just didn't feel like he wanted to be out there anymore. So, he gave it up.

Meanwhile, I jumped from job to job then ended up starting a HobbyTown USA business. I ran that for a few years before selling out.

During that time, I met a guy by the name of John. He became a friend of mine, and like me, he built remote control airplanes.

John was also a truck driver.

One night, John stopped by my house while I was working on an airplane, and I said to him, "well, I don't know what I'm gonna do anymore now that I've sold out of HobbyTown."

John said, "well, everybody wants you to open another hobby store."

"I can't open another hobby store for three years because I was under contract with HobbyTown. So, I've got to find something else to do for a while."

And then John came up with this bright idea. Be a truck driver.

I said, "yeah, I've done it before. Driven here and there by myself and with my brother."

"Well," he said, "I got to pick up a load tomorrow and take it over to Cleveland, Ohio, so why don't you ride with me? And if you like it, there you go. It'll give you a chance to check it out."

So, the next night I met John and we took off. Ran out through Milwaukee to Chicago and as we were coming out of Chicago, John said, "you ready to drive?"

I was like, *what?*

He said, "yeah, jump over here. Let's do it."

So, he did the same thing my brother did. He turned the cruise control on, kind of stood up and I jumped over there and started driving.

He sat next to me and had me downshift. And then he'd have me upshift. After I did that a few times he's like, "you got it. Just jump on 20 and run it all the way across. You'll be good."

I said, "okay."

So he crawled in the back, went to sleep, and I ran 20 all the way across Indiana and into Ohio.

Every once in a while, coming through a small town, I couldn't get the truck into gear, and John'd call from the back "give it more gas." And away I'd go.

We got into Cleveland, and John took over, got to the place, backed in and got out, while I slept for the return trip.

When we got back, I said, "yeah, I think I'll do that."

So, John told me to call around for companies that would send me for training.

I called around and found Swift Transportation. They offered a training program that sent you to a place to get your license. I'd go to this school for two weeks. After that, I'd be teamed with a Swift trainer for four weeks, then partnered with another student for another four weeks, and then I could drive solo.

I applied. Not long after, they called me back and said we can have you in the school on Monday. And I said, let's do it! Make it happen, captain.

So, I went to school. It was Fox Valley Technical College. They have a driving course that teaches you how to drive, and they help you get your license, and everything.

I also met a good friend of mine there, who started at the same time I did. We were two Wisconsin boys kind of going through it all together.

We also went through it really fast.

All the trainers said, "you guys got this."

So we jumped into a truck together—we'd gotten our licenses in four days—and practiced driving around town, backing up and whatever, just putting tons of miles on.

When our two weeks were up at the school, we went to Swift, which is up by Appleton, Wisconsin, and they paired each of us up with another trainer.

The trainers we got were also friends, so we would haul loads with each other. We did that for four weeks.

My Swift trainer was really good. Whenever you start with a new company it's hard to find a good trainer. People blame trainers for a lot. But you also gotta remember their truck is their home and they're letting you stay in it for a few weeks. It's hard on them, too.

I finished the course, came back, passed another driving test and was permitted to be a solo driver.

My buddy had gotten back from his training before me, so Swift gave him the truck we'd been using to drive around town a few weeks before.

Now it was my turn for a truck, and Swift said, we don't have another truck.

I was like, "Oh, okay. Now what?"

They searched and searched their computers and finally found one in Minneapolis. So they put a load on my buddy's truck, and me and him drove over to Minneapolis.

We pulled into their little terminal and there was an old Freightliner FLD. The keys were supposed to be on the dipstick.

I walked up to the truck and the windows were all busted and cracked, big chunks of the hood were broken, holes everywhere. It was terrible. This truck was in bad, bad shape.

But I messed around until I found the keys, unlocked the truck and threw all my stuff in there. I was so tired.

The truck started up, so I told my buddy we were good to go. He took off, and I crawled in the back. The truck didn't even have a mattress. Just bare wood. I threw my blankets and stuff down, laid on top all of that and went to sleep.

The next morning, I called up the terminal and said, "listen, I'm in the truck, but this thing is so bad it is not able to be legal."

"Well," they said, "the problem is we got to get it back here to Appleton to get the work done. Is there any way you can get it here?"

"Yeah, I probably can get it there, but I'm not going to go until tonight. I don't want to go through scales with this thing."

They said, "no problem. Don't even worry about a load or nothing, just bobtail all the way back."

So I waited until later that night, took off, got through all the scales, everything was closed, and ran her back to Appleton.

The next morning, I checked her into the shop, and they went through it, replaced the windshields, fixed a few things here and there. Got it roadworthy.

It was still an ugly, beat-up truck. But the thing is, these people invested a lot of time and money into training me and I was brand new. So, who am I to go to them and say, I need a new truck? I wasn't made that way. This is the truck I was given, and I'd make it work.

So they said, "Okay, we got a load you can pick up."

It was going to Pennsylvania. But I was so tired. So, I told them, "well, how about if I go pick up this load, run it through Chicago tonight, shut down, then get up early in the morning and have it to Pennsylvania midday?"

They agreed, so I went and picked up the load and took off.

When I got through Chicago, down to Gary, Indiana, I thought *this is where I'm going to shut it down.* So, I pulled into the Pilot truck stop in Gary.

Any truck driver reading this knows exactly the place I'm talking about.

The parking area is terrible. It is set up so badly that a truck can't go in and do a turnaround. There's not enough room.

But I pulled in anyway.

Across from me was a grassy hill next to a single parking spot. I thought, *okay, I'm gonna back in here.* Hopefully, there'd be enough room. I slid my tandems all the way forward, inched my nose back as far as I possibly could, got her in, shut her down, and went to sleep.

About an hour or so later I woke up to fiberglass crunching. I jumped up to see a truck backing down the left side of me, hitting my hood and mirror. I blew my horn a little bit and the guy stopped, got out, came back, looked at it and said, "Oh man, I'm so sorry."

I'm like, "it's all right, no problem." I got dressed and went out to help him get backed in. He had a beautiful truck. He just couldn't figure out which way to turn the steering wheel to get her back in there.

Finally, out of frustration, he just looked at me and said, "do you want to do it?"

I said, "sure" and jumped up in his truck. The interior was really fancy, all chrome and lit up.

I asked the guy if he minded if I jumped the curb right ahead of me. He agreed, so I just bounced up over the curb to give some more room and then zipped her right in there in one shot. The guy goes, "you're really good at backing up. Must've been doing this long time, huh?"

I said, "well, tell you the truth, today's my first solo day."

"And I hit you" he said, writing out his name and number for the insurance. We took pictures and I told him, "you know what? I don't even think there's going to be a problem here because there were cracks and missing chunks before you hit me. I don't think I'll need your name, but I'll keep it. The next time I go to a terminal, if anybody says something, I'll say, well, this is what happened."

He goes, "I appreciate that. My insurance is already pretty high."

Turned out the guy was an owner-operator.

With him safely parked next to me, I crawled back into my truck and went to sleep.

A few hours later, I wake up to an earthquake, the truck shaking and moving all around and I'm like, what in the hee-haw is going on here?! I looked out my front window and right across it was US Express.

Seems a US Express driver had pulled down the aisle, saw there was no place to park, and tried to turn. But when he turned, the tail end of his trailer bumper knocked off my hood, and now the bumper on his trailer was hooked to the bumper on my truck and the guy was just punching it and punching it, trying to get loose.

Everywhere, people were honking their horns. Finally, he gave up and got out.

After we got him untangled, I called up Swift to tell them what happened. I was actually pretty close to their terminal in Chicago, so they said, "well, can you get it there?"

I said, "I have no hood and I have no headlights either. But I'll see what I can do." So, I went into the store and bought a bunch of duct tape and rope and stuff, went back to the truck and we all pieced together that hood. Then with rope and more tape, we wrapped the whole truck to hold it together. It was the funniest looking thing.

There was one headlight that was still working, and I taped it onto the side of the hood.

As I was about to take off, the guy next to me who'd hit me the first time asked, "so you don't need my name anymore, do you?"

I just started laughing and said, "no, you're all good dude," and returned the piece of paper with his name and insurance.

It wasn't easy, but I got her to the Swift terminal, and when I drove up to the gate, the guys sitting by the front door just turned and stared. It must've been a pretty funny sight.

So, there I was for the rest of the day while they fitted a new hood and got everything else working. After that it wasn't that bad of a truck.

When they were done, and the truck was roadworthy, I called my dispatcher, told her the story, and she was like, "are you kidding me?"

I said, "nope, I couldn't make this up."

That was my first day at trucking, and that's how it all started.

I BREAK IT, I FIX IT

I started working fixing things when I was very young. I'm talking four or five-years-young. My parents had to hide their tools from me to keep me from tearing things apart. At first, they thought I was little Mr. Destruction. But I was actually trying to figure out how things worked. I took apart doors, disassembled hinges, doorknobs, even gutted a radio.

Then, when I reached nine or ten-years-old, my father was in a terrible car accident. Paralyzed with a broken neck, he was in and out of hospitals. My oldest brother, who'd moved out, came back home to run our 300+ acre farm, and the rest of us, when we were not in school, pitched in with the milking, the pigs, and the crops to keep the family going.

Now, my dad, who was a welder in the Army, did all the welding around the farm. And because I was the youngest, I followed him around, watching everything he did. When he wasn't looking, I would grab the welder and build all kinds of weird stuff.

So, while my dad was at the clinics, my older brothers were out doing all the field work, running the big machinery. When something broke, they'd bring the tractor or whatever, back to the house, grab something to eat, or take a nap, and I'd fix it. I'd weld the plowshares, repair the tires, or fix whatever else was broken. And that became my job growing up.

My dad did get better—it was quite a miracle, actually—and started working the farm some, but was never able to do all he'd done before.

When I was older, I joined a group of farm kids and formed a little mini bike gang.

My parents were pretty tight with their money. Instead of asking them to get me a mini bike like the other kids, I made one. I went out to the shop, grabbed some tubing we had laying around, and welded up my own mini bike frame. I found an old motor for it, fixed it up, then added an old banana seat and handlebars from a bent bicycle. The front tire, I nicked from a rusted-out wheelbarrow. The only thing I needed was a back tire with a sprocket that would drive the chain. And a clutch.

One Saturday, my dad took me out to this place called Dave's Small Engines. I told the guy what I needed, he handed me a clutch and some chain for about $10, then he sent me upstairs where he had some tires with sprockets.

I climbed the stairs, started digging through all the tires, and I found one that was a tractor tire with tractor tread. I have no idea what it came off of, but it had a sprocket—a very *big* sprocket. It was so cool! I manage to get it down the steps, showed it to the guy, and he said, "yeah, I don't think you want that one."

And I'm like, "why not?"

"Well, your gearing might be way off. There are actual mini bike back tires up there."

"Yeah, but this one's cool."

The guy shrugged, and so did my dad, who added, "you'll figure it out."

So, I put this thing together, and it was the coolest mini bike you've ever seen. Everybody else had these store-bought things. But mine was like a chopper with a banana seat and a big ol' tractor tire in the back. Sure, the other bikes could take off quicker, but mine had good top-end power and could hit 65 miles an hour. I used to run that thing all over the place, running up and down the roads between the neighbors' houses, just flying.

When I graduated from high school, I decided to go into auto-body work, and went to a tech school. The whole time I was there I was working as a welder too, making like 23 bucks an hour—right out of high school. I loved the workshop part of the autobody program, but the classroom part, I was like, you know, I just did high school. I really don't feel like sitting in more classrooms.

So, I went back to taking things apart. I tore apart engines, transmissions, all kinds of different things, then put them all back together and guess what? They all worked!

Then I started working for Schwinn Trucking, and got into an

accident while driving a Semi. I was thrown into the windshield, injured my shoulder, and temporarily lost the use of my
arm. When I got out of the hospital and gave my boss the slip
from the doctor, he asked if I'd be going on workman's comp. I
told him I didn't want to, I had one good arm. So, he introduced
me to the company's new computerized inventory system,
handed me a clipboard, and I started counting parts all around
the shop.

While I was counting parts and updating the computer, the shop
mechanic—who was drunk half the time—would be working on
something, just struggling and getting all upset. And I'd watch
him, and be like, *what is this guy doing?*

One time he was putting together a wheel hub, getting all frustrated. I walk over, and he's putting a bearing in backwards. So,
I helped him. Then I found him putting a seal in backwards and
helped again. Soon he started asking me for help, and I'd be
like, "sure, I'll do what I can." After all, I only had one good
arm at the time. But the guy must have thought I was a
mechanic because he started coming to me more often and with
more complicated problems. Finally, I said, "I'm not the
mechanic, here."

Still, he'd call me over to look at something else.

Well, the boss caught wind of this and asked me, "what are you
doing?" I told him I was being careful, even though my arm was
nearly 100%. But that wasn't what my boss wanted to know.

See, this guy and my boss would get into fights all the time, and
the guy'd get fired. But the next day the guy would just come
back to work like nothing happened.

Several days later, the boss saw this guy and me with our heads in another piece of machinery as I worked out what had been put in backwards or whatever. All of a sudden, he and the boss got into a big fight.

My boss said to the guy, "You know what, I'm done. Get your toolbox out of my shop. Don't ever come back here again. I don't want to hear from you. I don't want to see you. You're done."

Then he pointed at me. "Larry's my new mechanic."

I was like, *huh.*

The guy laughed and my boss walked up to me. "Larry, you want to be a mechanic?"

"Uhm...I really don't know too much about these trucks."

"You know how to fix stuff. You grew up on a farm. You know what you're doing. If you got questions, ask me."

So, I started doing just that, and he taught me a lot. He knew the old Mack trucks inside and out. Showed me how to rebuild everything. And once he showed me, I was good to do it again. That's the way I've always been.

Then I met another mechanic. He was top notch. Unbelievably good. He worked in another shop, but my boss would pay him cash to come in at night to rebuild blown engines.

But it got to be too much for him, between his fulltime job, family, and working on the side. So my boss said, "I'll have Larry tear down the engines, so when you get here, they're ready for you to just put back together."

So, I tore out the next blown engine, laid it all out, and had it ready for him. When the guy came in, I was getting ready to leave, and he asked, "do you want to learn how to do this?"

I said, "yeah, I'd love to."

"Good. That way I don't have to come back here."

So I stayed and worked, and he taught me how to rebuild a motor. The next day I came, did the final hookups, bolted everything onto the outside of the engine, and got it running.

My boss was like, "Wow, that was fast. We're gonna do it that way from now on."

A few days later, another motor needed to be rebuilt, so my boss talked to the mechanic, told him about the motor then said, "I'll have Larry tear it down for you."

The guy told him, "I've trained Larry."

My boss looked at me like *what?* I hadn't told him how I worked with him, and he taught me how to do it.

The mechanic kept talking. "See if he can handle the rebuild. If he has any questions, give him my cell phone number, and he can call me. If the problem is too big, I'll come in."

My boss said to me, "do it." So, I rebuilt the engine, and it worked. It worked real good.

The guy wasn't just a really good mechanic, he was a really good teacher, too. He taught me a lot about mechanics and how trucks work. He gave me an excellent education.

But now, these newer trucks have all these computer modules

and sensors. I have no skill with that stuff. Old school mechanical stuff, that I can make work.

I've actually thought about going back to Fox Valley tech school to learn the "new stuff" and getting the skills. It's a two-year course, I think, for truck mechanics. But I just don't see my life going in that direction.

Still, you never know.

If you drive 'em, you better be able to fix 'em. It's hard to survive, depending on others to fix your stuff when it breaks.

MY NEW TRUCK

A fter I finished training and got my CDL, Swift put me in a solo truck. It was not a pretty truck. The windows were broken, it had no mattress, there were cracks in the fiberglass. But it was all they had available, so I made it work.

I drove that truck for like four months. And every time I'd pass a Freightliner place, I'd stop and pick up pamphlets for new trucks, and when I came back to the office, I'd walk up behind my driving manager and drop them in front of him on his desk. He'd look up at me and I'd say, "Yup, I'll take that one right there."

Then we'd laugh.

Well, one day—I guess they thought I was doing well and was going to stick with it—Swift decided to give me a new truck.

So, I get a call from my driving manager. He says, "Hey dude. How would you like to have a brand-new Freightliner?"

"That's what I've been telling you about!"

"I can get you one."

"Okay. Where do I pick it up?" I was waiting for the punchline.

"First, I'll get you a load back to Green Bay. Then I'll get you another load out of Green Bay to Phoenix, Arizona, where there's a new truck waiting with your name on it. Zero miles."

"And the catch?"

"You'll need to take this other guy with you. He's just gone through training and needs a truck."

He paused.

I waited for the other shoe to drop.

"See…we've been trying to find this guy a truck for the last few days while he's been going on and on and on that it better be a new truck and it better be a nice truck. He's not my driver. But somehow, they put it on me to find him a truck. And the truck he's getting is *your* truck. But I don't want you to tell him that."

"Okay." No way was I going to say "no" to a new truck.

So, I deadheaded to Green Bay, picked up a load and headed over to the yard to pick up the soon-to-be owner of my less-than-nice truck.

Earlier in the day, I'd shot a message to the yard saying I was on my way and to tell the new guy to be well-rested because I'd be nearly out of hours when I got there, and he'd need to drive a shift.

Then, thirty minutes out, I sent another message to have the guy waiting outside and ready. My logbook was running, and I didn't have time to waste.

They promised he'd be ready and waiting outside.

So, I roll up and there's this guy sitting on the curb. I said, "Hey dude. Ready for a ride to Arizona?

He says, "Yep"

"I'm Larry. You ready to go? Where's your bags?"

He looks around. "Oh, Oh yeah, okay. Um, I'll have to get the shuttle guy to take me back over to the hotel. I left them there."

"What? I gotta go. My logbook is running. Didn't they tell you to be ready to go?"

"Yeah, I'm standing here, right?"

I went inside, yelled about it a little bit, and they got somebody to run him to the hotel to get his bags.

The guy was already on the wrong foot with me.

Finally, he was loaded in my (soon to be his) truck, and on the road. He's looking around disapprovingly at the interior of my truck while I'm trying to explain that he'll be taking over when my hours run out. "So, if you're at all tired or anything else, you need to get in the back and go to sleep. You got a sleeping bag?"

"No."

"Do you have a pillow or anything?

"No."

"Well, what do you plan to sleep on in this new truck?"

Silence.

"Didn't you just come out of a trainer's truck?"

Now, it's commonly understood when you're in another person's truck, and they're driving, you're sleeping in a bottom bunk, which is probably their bunk, too. So, you bring a sleeping bag to lay on top of their bedding and sleep in the bag. And you never use the other driver's pillows. No one wants you drooling on their pillows or farting in their sheets!

This guy had no clue.

Eventually, he went in the back and sat there talking and talking and talking. I finally interrupted. "Dude, you going to be okay to drive tonight, right?"

"Oh yeah, probably."

"Look, you're not training anymore. You're a truck driver now. Get some sleep so you can drive tonight."

He closed the curtain, it got nice and quiet, and I tried to drive real smooth for the guy so he could sleep.

When we got down to Iowa, my hours ran out. I opened the curtain a bit and said "Hey dude, we're going to be pulling over in a few minutes. Time to get yourself going so we can switch over."

He sat up all bleary-eyed.

I pulled over, ready to switch, and he was still sitting there.

"You need a cup of coffee or something? What's going on here?"

"Oh, I really didn't fall asleep at all. I was reading."

"Why didn't you sleep?"

"It's a good book."

"You know, we have to keep this truck rolling. This load was put on us because we were going to be a team and it has to be there fast. There's no time for stopping and sleeping and stuff."

So, the guy got into the driver's seat and took over.

I stayed up a little while because I wanted to see if he could actually drive. He got to the highway, got on, and I was like, "All right. I'm gonna go back and sleep. But I'm leaving the curtains open. If you need anything, you just holler."

He agreed, so I went back there and fell dead asleep.

About two hours later, I'm awake and the truck is stopped. It's not moving. And I'm like, *what's going on?* I jump up, look around. He's not in the truck!

We're parked in a rest area, so I put some clothes on, got out and started walking toward the building thinking the guy had to go to the bathroom and I should check on him, make sure he's not sick or something.

Then I spot him. He's sitting on a picnic table smoking a cigarette, just sitting there, and guess what? He's reading a book!

I walk up to him. "Hey, what are you doing?"

"Oh, oh, hey Larry, you woke up?"

"Ah, yeah. What are we doing here?"

"Oh man, I got tired. I got, real tired. I just didn't feel it was safe. So, I decided to pull over and let you sleep."

"Well if you're so tired, why would you pull over just to let me sleep? Why aren't *you* sleeping?"

"Ah, I was wanting to get back to my book."

This guy was on my last nerve. I said "Dude, get back in that truck, get back in that bunk." Then I took the book from him. "And you'll get this when we get to Arizona."

Back in the truck, he went to the bunk and I drove off of his logbook. (Statute of limitations has expired, so I can admit it, now.)

I drove all night listening to this guy snore. I was so aggravated I didn't want to see him. I didn't want to talk to him. So, I kept going.

But by about five, six o'clock in the morning anger wasn't enough to keep me awake. I was falling out.

I yelled for the guy and he stuck his head out between the curtains. "What? What?"

"Get out here and do some driving."

I got pulled into a truck stop and the guy is still sitting on the bunk rubbing his eyes, "Man, I didn't get any sleep last night."

That put me right over the edge. "Don't you give me this 'you haven't gotten any sleep'. You snored all night."

He blinked. "Oh, I just don't think it's safe for me to drive being so sleepy."

I got out of the cab, went into the truck stop, picked up some coffee and some NoDoz (energy boost) pills, went back and closed the curtain on the guy who was still in the bunk. "And I don't want to see you until we get to Arizona.

"What if I got to go to the bathroom?"

I tossed an empty soda bottle in his direction, grabbed the wheel and drove straight through to Arizona.

After dropping off my load, I pulled into the yard where I'm to pick up my new truck. It is the biggest truck lot I've ever seen in my life. There're signs on all the light poles labeling each section like an airport, and dozens of people who do nothing but drive around golf carts transporting truckers back and forth from their trucks to the terminals.

I'm loading my bags into one of the carts when the guy finally climbs out of the truck and I kind of apologize to him a little bit. "You know, you're a professional, now. You have got to learn that you got to drive the truck. That's all there is to it."

"Yeah, I'm sorry about that. I was so tired."

I hand him his book and climb in next to the golf cart driver. The guy piles into the back and we head for a little mobile office surrounded by hundreds of new trucks.

The man inside the little office asks for my paperwork and the truck number, then hands me the keys and said, "here ya go. Your brand-new truck is right out there. Do a walk-around, sign this sheet then bring it back to me."

As I'm heading for the door, I hear the guy who I brought down say, "I'm here for a truck, too."

"I don't see your name on the list. You got a truck number?"

"Uh, no. They didn't give me one."

The guy yelled for me. "Hey Larry! Can I use your phone? I need to call up there and find out what's going on."

I turned around and said, "I can tell you what's going on buddy. You're getting my truck."

"But your truck is old!"

"Dude, you don't even know how to drive. What makes you think they're going to give you a brand new, $100,000 truck? You need to drive what they give you. Do a good job and maybe they'll give you a new one."

"Oh, but I got to call them. This isn't right. Can I borrow your phone?"

He'd asked to borrow my phone a couple of times before and I'd always said no. But this time, I tossed it to him. Let my Driving Manager, who stuck me with this guy, explain it. I had a new truck to look at.

Inspection complete, bags loaded, and paper signed, I returned to the mobile office where the guy was just ending his call. He handed me back my phone. "I guess I'm getting your truck," he said. "But I told them it's gotta be washed because it's dirty."

I handed him the keys. "Ya know, dude, they gotta wash bay here."

We did a quick walk around my old truck and I showed him a few things to pay attention to, especially the air dryer. When it would cycle it would make this eerie Friday the 13th kind of sound. Not something to worry too much about, and not something I was going to miss.

Then I climbed into my brand-new zero-miles truck and took off, zipping through a bunch of lanes. When I was sure he wasn't following, I drove all the way to the very back corner of this humungous lot, found a spot and parked.

Then I fell face-down, fully clothed, on the plastic-wrapped mattress and went dead asleep, until…

BOOM!

I sat straight up.

And then I heard an old familiar sound, that eerie Friday the 13th sound.

I parted the curtains and looked out my passenger side window, and that dude was parked right next to me, staring into my truck. As soon as he saw me, he yelled out "Heeyy, Laarrrryy!"

I was like, *oh my goodness, are you kidding me?* I opened up my window. "What can I do for you?"

"Well, I was just wondering, you know, I'm hooking up to this trailer, and I need—"

I said, "Dude, I don't have time for this. I have to leave. I have a load to pick up, right now." Completely lied. But I had to get away from him before I did some serious damage. "And, I'm supposed to run over to the truck stop right down the road and get something for this truck. They don't have it here." Again, a complete lie.

"Oh, you mean the TA down there? 'Cause they got a truck wash and I want to get the truck washed"

I said, "They got a truck wash here."

"Aw yeah, but they told me I could take it to the TA. So, I'm going to follow you."

You don't want to know what I was thinking.

I was bobtailing, so I peeled out of there for the exit gate and got in line to leave. There was probably, I don't know, eight trucks or so ahead of me, and here comes that guy up behind me real fast. But he had no trailer. He pulls up right behind me, pops his brakes, jumps out and comes running up to me.

I open my door and he says, "Hey, I uhm, I uhm just flipped over my trailer.

"You *what*?"

"Yeah. It's laying back there. On its side. Do you think if I just leave it anybody'll know?"

What could I say? I really didn't think the guy was *that* stupid.

So I pointed up to the lightbulbs. "See those lights. They each have a camera. You bang something, they know it. You flip a trailer, they'll find you."

He looked so forlorn I asked the one question I shouldn't have. "So, what happened?"

His face brightened some. "Well, I took off after you. Peeled out real fast. I turned, and when I turned, the next thing I heard was a big *boom*. I looked back and the trailer was...it was going nose down, and then it rolled, and then it was on its side."

It was hard to keep from laughing. "Dude, if you don't turn around and go back there and go find somebody to help you with this situation, you might as well park the truck here, get on a Greyhound bus and go home because you're going to be fired."

"Oh, you think so?"

Maybe he was *that* stupid. "Yeah, I know so."

He headed back to his truck, and I started thinking. That big bang that woke me up...was that him slamming his truck into the trailer? Had he backed into it so fast and so hard that the fifth wheel hit then bounced back before it closed? Then, when he peeled out after me and turned, it just came right off his truck.

I laughed all the way to the truck-stop, and then slept there.

The next day I returned to the terminal to send a message into my fleet manager. I said, "I am taking today to sleep. I drove the whole way here. That guy you sent with me is an idiot. I will contact you when I get up and I don't want another load put on me until then."

Twelve hours or so later, and back to my old self, I called my fleet manager to tell him I was heading out. He said, "Well, that load you took down, it's headed for California, and that guy you took down there with you was supposed to deliver it. But he messed up or something."

I said, "Yeah, he tipped the load over."

"Oh no, it wasn't that load. He mistakenly hooked up to the wrong trailer, and now they won't let him go out of there." I really should not have laughed. "So, until that's all taken care of, we need somebody to grab the load to California."

When I got back to Appleton, three weeks later, I asked my driver manager, "Hey, that guy I took down to Arizona, how's he doing?"

"He's still not home. We routed him back here with a load and plans to put him in more classes. But he'll only drive two or three hours then calls to say…"

"…that he's so tired. It's just not safe for him to drive."

We both laughed.

Six weeks later the cops found my old truck in Iowa, abandoned, the guy and his book nowhere to be found. Guess he finally took my advice and grabbed that Greyhound bus.

TWO SEMI ACCIDENTS

I have been in two accidents with a semi.

The second accident was when I was working as an independent trucker.

I was in Wisconsin coming through Appleton to a traffic light, there. The light changed to yellow, and if you're a truck driver you know you don't have the same rules as a car. If you're driving a car coming to an intersection and the light turns yellow before you hit the crosswalk, that means stop.

A truck requires more distance.

When driving a truck, there's a point of no return that's much farther back than the crosswalk. If you try stopping within 50 feet of a stop sign while going 35 to 45 miles an hour, you'll be halfway into the intersection before your wheels stop rolling. So, a lot of times, it's better to go through the yellow than it is to try to stop and cause problems.

Well, the light turned yellow just as I was coming up to it. There was nothing I could do, so I just kept going. Then, when I was about halfway across the intersection, it turned red—it was a really quick light.

As soon as the light turned red, a car that was sitting at the light took off. The guy didn't look left or right, wasn't looking at the intersection, he just hit the gas.

I swerved as best I could, caught the end of his front bumper with my truck, ripped it off, and wrinkled his fender a little bit.

When I came to a stop, I went back to check on the guy and asked, "you okay?"

He's like, "yeah, I'm fine."

I called the police, and of course somebody had to come over and say "that truck went through a red light. He was in the intersection when it turned red."

I'd already told that to the cop. There's nothing you can do when this happens and you're in a truck.

So I told the guy whose car I'd hit, "don't worry about it. We'll take care of it. That's why we have insurance." I gave the guy my information, patched up his car enough so he could drive it home, and told him to take it to a garage and see what he wants to do. It was a piece-of-junk car.

He called me the next day and said he took his car—it was a Hyundai—to a buddy who has a garage and he said it'd be like $3,000.

I asked, "What year is this car?"

I don't remember exactly what he said, but the car was about 15 years old. So, I said, "Let me think about this."

After looking up the car's blue book value, I called him back. I said "Listen, I'm not going to do this with you. The blue book on the car comes to about $1200. I understand there was a disruption in your life and everything else, but I'm not going to pay $3,000 to some buddy of yours so you guys can junk the car and spend the money. I'm not playing that game. So, here's what I'll do: I'll give you $2,000 if you sign a form saying I'm not liable for anything else."

The guy said, "Well, you know, there's my time."

"We can either do it my way or we can let the insurance company deal with it. I guarantee you they're going to total the car and pay the lowest blue book value possible."

He agreed.

So I contacted my lawyer, got the form from him, then met with the guy.

He read the form and started complaining about his back hurting.

"Listen," I said. "I don't want to hear it. If you don't want to do it this way, you don't get the money." I grabbed the form from him and put the $2000 check back in my pocket. "My insurance company will contact you."

I started to leave, and the guy yelled, "Whoa, wait a minute, wait a minute. Ok, I'll sign."

So he signed the form, I gave him the money, then told him,

"You know, you really shouldn't try to shake people down. One of these times you're going to run into somebody who's not gonna like it too much." I just walked away.

It was worth it to pay the extra bucks and not turn the claim into the insurance because it would have really raised my rates, and when you're an independent trucker, keeping a low rate is important if you want to make any money.

My first accident happened when I was working for Schwinn Transport driving a '68 Mack Cruiseliner cabover truck.

One day I showed up for work and another driver had grabbed my truck. So I went into the office and they started trying to figure out where my truck was. The boss finally figured out it was the driver who arrived a little bit before me. The boss yelled at him saying "you can't just jump in any truck", and then told me to take that driver's truck.

I didn't know anything about this guy's truck, what kind of upkeep he did or anything. But I jumped in his truck and took off, already late to do my runs.

Driving to my first pickup, I was running pretty fast when I came to a stop sign and it seemed like my brakes were not operating properly, not grabbing the best. I thought, okay, maybe they needed an adjustment or something. This was an older truck, so you had to adjust the brakes once in a while.

The roads were all wet and slimy with snow and salt, and I'd have to crawl underneath the truck to make the adjustment. So I figured when I got up to Chilton, where I would be unloaded inside a building, I'd do the brake adjustment there.

I was pulling a loaded food-grade tanker. Tankers, especially food tankers, are tricky to haul because they don't have baffles in them. It's just a big open tube.

A fuel tanker or a sludge tank, something that hauls a non-food grade product, has what's called baffles—basically half walls—welded inside. Half the baffles come down from the ceiling, the other half come up from the floor and they're staggered. And they'll drill holes in them. So if you have to hit the brakes pretty hard, the liquid kinda hits those walls and keeps the liquid from building momentum by disrupting the flow.

But food-grade trailers don't have those.

I'm running up towards Chilton, the tanker is about three-quarters full. Coming out of Kiel, I was about 75 feet from a driveway when I saw a truck hauling one of those big construction office trailers. He was driving toward the end of the driveway. I was coming down the road, and the guy pulled out right in front of me. He never stopped. He never even looked at me. He just pulled right out into the road!

I slammed on the brakes, swerved as hard as I could into the empty oncoming traffic lane and he just took off.

Well, I had to downshift a bunch of gears, get myself back onto my side of the road, and I was pretty upset with this guy.

So, I took off after him.

But there was a slight uphill and I was three-quarters loaded, so I was not gonna get going fast.

My plan was to blow my horn at the guy—like that'll teach him, you know. Truthfully, I don't know what I was thinking, but that was my intention.

So, I was trying to catch up with him. I could see him up ahead, and I was getting closer and closer and closer until I realized w*hoa, I'm really catching this guy fast.*

I started to brake.

And when I started to brake the liquid in the back started to move. You just can't slam on your brakes with a near-full tanker truck. It'll throw you around.

So, I'm trying to brake lightly but there was no way I could stop in time. The brakes just were not up to standard and I knew I wasn't going to be able to stop.

The guy was just sitting there, right in the middle of the road!

It was two lanes, one lane in each direction. And he was just stopped right there in the middle. Just stopped!

As I got closer, I saw a right turning lane.

If the guy was planning a right turn, he would be in the right turning lane, right? But there were no lights working on the back of the trailer. No taillights, no stop lights, no turn signals to indicate his direction.

So, I figured he was making a left, and shot into the right lane. The lane was narrow so I had to put my tires kind of up on the shoulder a little bit throwing snow everywhere as I'm trying to slow down the best I can.

I got within probably 25 feet of this guy and he turned right in front of me.

I mean, when I was a good quarter-mile away, coming up to him, he didn't move, then at the very last second (I think he saw me in the mirror) he cut me off.

I turned the wheel as fast as I possibly could to the left. And it was just no good.

I ran right into the rear end of that office trailer.

In my cab, the seatbelt was missing. Some of these trucks that Schwinn had didn't have seatbelts. This truck did have one at one time, but now it didn't so I went flying forward, and with my left shoulder and the left side of my head smashed the windshield and busted it right out.

On my way through the windshield, my legs got pinned under the steering wheel, so I reached back, grabbed the dash, pulled myself back into the truck and kept steering. I was all over the road. When I got back on my side of the road, I popped the brakes, finally the truck came to a stop.

The office trailer, which had become disconnected from its metal frame, was now flying through the air toward the intersection where a van sat. That trailer sailed right over the top of the van, scared the Dickens out of the people inside I'll tell you that much, and landed in a ditch.

Someone called the police.

A cop arrived, talked to everybody, one by one, in his police car, and saved me for last.

But just before the cop got to me, a guy in a pickup truck showed up and started talking to the driver of the other semi.

When the cop got out of his car and opened the door for the last witness to exit, the guy from the pickup called out, "I'm the owner of this company. I was at the job site this truck just came from. I checked his lights right before he left."

So the cop called the guy over to take his statement.

I had already called my boss and told him, "Hey, I need some electrical testing equipment and a camera up here" I'd gone over and looked at that wiring, and that wiring had not been working for a long time. It was all corroded and rusted and broken. I want pictures of all this.

When the owner got out of the cop car, the cop called me over. I sat in the car and asked, "what's up?"

"Well," he said, "I just want to let you know that you're at fault."

"How am I at fault?" I hadn't even told my side of what happened.

"You're going to get a ticket for following too closely."

"Following too closely? I was way back there when the guy was stopped in the middle of the road. No signal. No brake lights. I had no idea what he was doing. Was he just stopped? Was he turning? By the time I realized I had to take evasive action, the guy cut me off."

The cop continued. "You hit him in the rear end, so you were following too closely."

"You're not even taking my statement. I want an investigation team out here."

"Nope. Tow trucks are on their way, and we're not tying the scene up any longer. This stuff's going to be all hauled off..." blah, blah, blah...

I just sat there, frustrated.

Finally, two guys from Schwinn showed up with a tow truck of their own and another truck cab.

By now, my arm was starting to hurt more and more.

The Schwinn guys pulled my busted truck out with the tow truck, then motioned to the other truck cab, "well, here ya go, Larry."

I was trying to crank the dolly and said, "dude, I can't feel my left arm. I don't think I should be driving. I think I should go to the hospital.

Suddenly the cop chimed in "you need an ambulance?" I'm like, "no, I don't need no ambulance. I'll go to the doctor myself." I had a few choice words for that cop.

By the time the Schwinn guy with the camera and testing equipment got there, they'd already loaded what remained of the trailer onto a flatbed. The other half was already gone. I couldn't even take pictures.

So, I went back to the shop with the tow truck driver and called my wife to take me to the hospital. I sat there in the waiting room talking to my boss. "You know," I said, "I'm telling you right now, I was not at fault with this. They're going to come after you to pay for stuff. Then there's the insurance. I'm telling you right now, I'm going to fight this." He was like, "yeah, whatever."

After a bunch of x-rays and tests, it turned out I had a stinger injury.

A stinger is what you get when a joint is hit really hard and the body basically shuts off the nerves to that limb. You can't feel anything in that limb. Then in a couple of days everything'll come back. But until it does, you really can't use that limb. It happens a lot in football games when players hit each other really hard.

The doctor seemed certain everything would start coming back in three to five days but wanted me to take off a couple weeks.

So, I went back to the shop and told my boss. He asked, "Oh, is this gonna be a workman's comp claim?"

I said, "No, I don't want it to be. You got something for me to do? I'll do it.

He said he did, and I inventoried parts for the next few weeks.

Well, my court date came up. They pulled me into a little room with the assistant district attorney and said, "Well, you know, you're here for your court appearance and if you accept two points and pay $200, we will give you this ticket. Or you can accept four points and pay $75 and will give you this other ticket."

They'll always try to make a deal to get you to sign off so they can close the case without messing around.

I said, "No, I'm not doing anything. I was not at fault for this. I want this clearly dropped."

"That isn't going to happen."

"Well, it *is* going to happen. I'll take it to court."

When I got back, my boss asked me what happened. "Well," I told him, "I hired an attorney and I'm going to be fighting it."

They were already after him for money for the accident site cleanup. They'd even put a price on that ratty office trailer.

So my attorney went to work, talking to the different people who'd been at the scene.

One of those people was the construction company owner, and this is how we got him.

My attorney went over to this guy's business and approached the guy's secretary. "I would like to speak to your boss about the accident that happened over on the highway."

"Oh yeah, yeah. He's on a phone call. But right after that, you could talk to him."

While waiting, my attorney continued talking to the secretary, "You seem to remember this accident."

"Yeah, I was here and the boss was in his office in a meeting. "My phone rang, it was the driver. He was all frantic and needed to talk to the boss real quick. I asked him what was going on. He said he was just in an accident. So I ran back into the office, told the boss, and he picked up the phone. No sooner was I back at my desk when he went storming out of here and peeled out of the parking lot."

"So, your boss was here in his office all morning, correct?"

"Oh yeah, yeah. He had meetings and other things. But yeah, he was here all morning."

When the guy walked out of his office, my attorney introduced himself.

"I already gave my statement," the guy said.

"I understand. I just have a few clarifying questions."

They stepped into the guy's office, and my attorney laid the trap. "So, in your statement, you said you were at the job site and you inspected the trailer to make sure the lights worked properly before the driver pulled out. Is that correct?"

The guy nodded.

"Then why did I just have a conversation with your secretary who said you were in the office, tied up in meetings and paperwork all morning, and you didn't leave your office until the driver called to report the accident?"

The guy got real quiet.

My attorney continued. "This is your opportunity to come clean because I'll subpoena your secretary."

The guy showed my attorney the door.

On his way out, my attorney handed the secretary his summary of her statement and asked if it was correct. She agreed it was and, so that "all the "i"'s could be dotted and "t"'s crossed", she signed the paper at his request.

My attorney's next stop was the district attorney's office. He showed him the secretary's signed statement, told him how the guy lied, and the district attorney said he would look into it.

A couple of weeks later, just a few days before our first court appearance, my attorney contacted the D.A. again, but he refused to drop the case.

We were going to court. But my attorney was certain he had all the proof needed to get the case dismissed.

So, I met him at the courthouse for our court appearance. He was on the phone in the lobby and asked me to get the courtroom number from the clerk. So, I headed into the clerk of courts, explained what I needed, and the lady couldn't find my name on her docket. She went to her computer, messed around some, came back and said, "Oh, well, we're seeing here that it's been dismissed."

I'm like, *what?*

I found my lawyer. He was still on the phone but turned to me and asked, "which courtroom?"

I said, "they dismissed it."

"Are you kidding me?" He hung up the phone, walked into the clerk of courts, talked to them, came back out, and oh was he mad.

He stormed up to the district attorney's office. I followed him right into the guy's office. They were already yelling back and forth, and the D.A. said, "I didn't really care about it. So I dropped it."

"You dropped it because I had evidence this guy lied. That was your main reason."

The D.A. shrugged.

So, my lawyer called down to the clerk of courts and asked which courtroom the case was supposed to be heard in. They told him. He asked if the judge was available. The clerk said he was available because the case had just been dismissed that day.

So, my attorney looked at the D.A. and said, "I'm going to have a chat with the judge and see what he has to say about it."

The D.A. jumped up, suddenly all interested.

So, we went into the judge's chambers. My attorney told the judge all about the case and stuff. Finally, the judge looked at the D.A. and asked, "Is this true?"

"Well, the construction company owner who was supposed to testify said he couldn't be in town. I really don't see this as a big thing, so I just dismissed it. Why waste the court's time?"

As the D.A. continued to talk, my lawyer called the construction company and asked for the owner. The secretary put him through. When the owner got on the line my attorney put him on speakerphone and said, "I'm thinking about, uh, coming in and talking to you about a construction job that I have planned. Are you available today? And the guy's like, "Yeah, I'll be in the office all day. Stop in."

The judge interrupted, identified himself and asked, "Weren't you supposed to be in court today to testify?"

You could hear the guy slap his own forehead.

The judge kept talking. "Here's what's going to happen. You're going to get in your car and come straight to the courthouse as fast as you possibly can, and you are going to come directly to my chamber. If you don't show up, I'm going to hold you in contempt."

So, we sat there and waited, and sure enough, the guy showed up. He admitted he was nowhere near the job site. He did not inspect the trailer lights or wiring, and he gave false information to the police.

Then the judge looked at me and said, "I'm sorry to waste your time, Larry. We will be dismissing all charges."

My attorney interrupted. "That's great, but I have to charge Larry for all the time I spent running around. He's going to get a big bill for absolutely nothing when I've been trying to tell the D.A. that the construction company owner has been lying all along."

The judge looked at the D.A. who began making more excuses.

The judge turned back to me and said, "You send your lawyer's bill to the district attorney and it'll be taken care of."

I didn't have to pay a dime, and my attorney got paid his full rate.

The next day, I showed up for work, and told my boss, "Well, I just got all the charges dismissed."

He just looked at me like, *really?*

I said, "Yup, everything was dropped, all charges dismissed. I am not at fault."

"Well, that's a little late. My insurance paid the guy out a few days ago."

I called my attorney and told him the news. He said, "I'm telling you right now, that's what the whole stall tactic was about. Once the insurance paid out, the owner didn't care about the charges being dismissed."

Seems the guy not only got paid for the trailer but for hauling it all away, too.

Long story short, the judge made another call, threw the words "insurance fraud" around, my boss got his money back, and everything got resolved.

That was the worst accident I've ever gotten into. I hope it stays that way.

SNOW, ICE AND WIND

I went to a truck driving school in Wisconsin, at the Fox Valley Technical College; they're the best I've encountered. I've been a trainer, and I've trained people from different trucking schools, and I'm telling ya, Fox Valley taught me a lot of things that kept me out of trouble.

Once a big backhoe fell off a trailer in front of me, and I was able to stop because of the training I had at Fox Valley.

Then there was the guy who drove off a mountain out in Idaho.

In Chicago, I had a car come right across the front of me and smash into a wall.

There's been a few more like those and every time, it's come back to my training and learning how to drive.

People often ask me, what's the worst thing in trucking? Rain, hail, snowstorms?

My second answer is wind. When you're hauling a big box

behind you, and you get a bad crosswind, that's all she wrote. If you can look out your side mirror and read the lettering on the side of your trailer, you know it's windy. Just hang onto her, keep her going, and get out of that wind.

My first answer to what's the worst thing in trucking? Ice. Ice storms are the worst. Snow doesn't bother me too much. It's ice.

One time I was heading north out of Illinois towards Madison and hit some ice. It was just pure ice. We were all coming to a stop 'cause a car went in a ditch, the tow truck was blocking part of the road. We are also on a slight hill. I saw what was coming, so I pulled onto the shoulder and grabbed the rumble strips. It was so slippery the tow truck guy, who was right up ahead of me trying to walk around his truck and do his job, just kept slipping and falling on his butt.

When they finally cleared the accident and everything, they made us move on. Since I was on rumble strips, I was able to get going, but the other trucks just started spinning.

Rolling forward, I looked back in my mirror. The trucks all started jack-knifing on the little hill and a couple of them sliding into ditches. It was pretty bad.

But I think the worst one I've ever had was going up through Michigan on the highway that rides right along the Lake, and it was snowing and icy. It was bad.

I was giving the semi in front of me 200 to 300 feet of distance 'cause she was sliding. You know you're sliding because you can feel it in your butt. That is the first place you feel when you start the slide. It feels like you're twisting in the seat, but you're not. It's a funny feeling.

So the guy in front of me kept breaking loose, and every time he did, he'd hit the brakes. I started yelling at him on the radio, "stop hitting the brakes. You're going to jack-knife, stop it, stop it." He didn't answer me back. I guess he didn't have a radio or whatever.

He just kept on going.

We came over a bridge, probably doing 30 to 40 miles per hour and the guy hit more ice. He started to slide, laid on the brakes, and went straight into a jackknife right in front of me.

My training kicked in. What Fox Valley taught was wherever you are looking is where you go. If you see an accident ahead of you, don't look at the accident, look at where you want to go and don't take your eyes off of that spot no matter what the truck is doing. If you're sliding or whatever, always look at the spot where you want to be.

So, the guy was jack-knifing really bad in front of me and began blocking the whole highway. I tapped the brakes a little bit and started to slide. I let off the brakes and saw there was an on-ramp alongside the guy so I headed for the ditch between the on-ramp and the highway, steering very slowly.

His truck started pointing across the highway, and as soon as I went off the shoulder and hit that on-ramp, I started to steer back real gently. The rumble strips grabbed me a little bit and I was able to steer and shot right around the back end of the guy's semi.

By now, his trailer was all sideways across the highway, his truck jack-knifed in the ditch, and I just rode the rumble strips back on the highway.

In my mirror, all I could see was headlights crashing into this guy. Cars spinning around. It was a mess.

I slowed way down. You just touch the gas and you started spinning. There were lights up ahead of me, so I kept going.

In probably half a mile I started going uphill. I was maybe going 10 to 15 miles an hour. As I crested the hill and started down the other side, I could see the flashing lights on a police car. I just pushed in the clutch, letting her roll and feathering the brakes, trying to slow her down as best I could.

I rolled right up alongside the cop who was babysitting a FedEx double laid over in a ditch. He opened his window and yelled, "yeah?". He was kind of aggravated 'cause I just stopped in the middle of the road. He didn't know that no one was gonna be coming behind me. I said, "Hey, a huge accident happened right behind me, the whole highway is messed up. Cars all piled into a jack-knifed truck."

He was like, "Oh yeah. Just came over the radio. EMS is on the way."

I just kept on going, and finally got her through there.

If you're going to be a truck driver, you'll get a lot of tense situations like that.

Some will even scare the pants off you once in a while.

Good training pays off. It takes a gentle touch and always looking where you want to be. ...good advice for lots of situations.

BUDDY THE TRUCKER KITTY

I like kitty cats. A lot of people have dogs that they bring on the trucks with them. But I like kitty cats, always have.

When I was young, I had an Uncle Bob. He wasn't really my uncle. To tell you the truth, I'm not sure what he was. I don't even think he was my dad's uncle. But he had a big farm out in Idaho where my parents are from.

Anyway, Uncle Bob was a farmer and he'd always ask me what I wanted to be when I grew up.

We lived on a farm, too, so I said, I'm going to be a farmer.

Then he'd asked me, what are you gonna raise? You gonna have cows? Pigs?

I said, Nope. I'm going to be a kitty farmer.

He just looked at me like, *what?*

And I said I'm going to raise cats.

Everybody has always picked on me about that, all my life. I was going to have a cat farm. But I have always liked cats. I think they're cool.

So, when I was trucking with Swift and spending a lot of time doing over-the-road, coming home about every three weeks, my ex-wife and my girls went out and bought me a cat for my birthday.

When I got home, they gave me this little kitten who I named Buddy.

I'm not a great namer of things as everybody should know. If my wife wasn't in the hospital when the kids were born, they probably would've grown up as "Kid One" and "Kid Two". Though it would've been kind of hard for her not to be there, you know?

Anyway, the cat stayed at home for about a month to grow up a little bit and get on regular food, then I was to take her along to live in the truck with me. I didn't know how it was going to work. But I thought I'd give it a try.

Buddy was a Markese Calico, and it took about a month for her to get used to everything, the truck constantly moving and stuff. Then she became so chill and just loved it.

She'd run around, jump up on the dash and just sit there watching the cars pass, the other trucks or whatever. She'd stare at the people as they went by, and the people would look over like, well, there's a cat! It was kinda different. Nobody really had cats. People had dogs, but no one had cats.

Buddy was weird. She was almost like a dog because you could say, "Buddy, come here" and she'd come to you. That's not normal for a cat. Usually, cats have an attitude and do what they want to do. But Buddy was different.

We had a good time in the truck, but when we would park at a truck stop or someplace, and there was somebody next to us who had a dog, that cat would mess with that dog to no end.

I would be in the back, sleeping, and you would hear a dog nearby just barking and barking and barking. Then you'd hear some guy yelling at his dog to shut-up. I would look up and there was Buddy, sitting on one of the front seats, slowly peeking her head up to the window.

In the truck next to us was the dog, nose plastered to the window, staring, waiting.

Buddy would slowly raise her head, then jump at the window.

And a dog would just go nuts barking.

Buddy would jump back down and sit there and hide.

Then the dog's owner would start yelling again.

And I'd sit there, and the cat would look at me and then do it again.

Buddy also had a leash that I kept right by the door. When I'd get in and out of the truck, I would leave the door open, and that cat would not jump out. She would just sit on my seat and I would be opening my doors, sliding my tandems, parking the truck, my door cracked or kinda open. And she would just stay right on the seat.

When I was finished, I'd grab the leash, snap it onto her collar, and she'd jump up on my shoulder, settle across my neck, and we'd find a grassy area. I'd take her off my shoulders and just kinda hold onto the leash, and she would run around and jump through the grass.

Other truckers watching this would be like "that's a cat!"

"Yeah, cats are cool."

Buddy listened so well that one time, I decided to take her off the leash to just let her run and see what she'd do.

So I disconnected the leash, put her down into this little field where the grass was probably a foot tall or so, and oh man, she took off running, jumping all around, just going crazy and having a ball. I sat there for like five minutes, letting her go, seeing her every once in a while, jumping around.

Then I called her, and she came right back, sat down and just looked at me. So, I'd say "go." And she'd take off again and run around. She got really good at it.

Eventually, I stopped putting her on a leash, and I would just let her run. Whenever she got a little far away, I'd yell at her, and she'd come right back to me. She wasn't a normal cat, but she was my buddy who lived in the truck with me.

I remember this one time... I was driving a classic truck that had mirrors with posts that came off the top of the door and there were two connecting posts that formed like an "A". I was parked, getting loaded, and I had my window cracked, like three, four inches.

A worker came out, told me I was loaded, so I pulled forward, closed my doors, and went in to get my paperwork. I had closed the driver's side door, but I didn't think about the window being open.

Walking back out, I wasn't paying attention, and I just jumped into the truck, put it in gear, and took off.

Coming out the driveway, I yelled for Buddy. She'd always run out and sit on my lap or jump up onto the dash. But she didn't come. I turned onto the street, and I'm looking around, checking out my bunk in the back. And I'm like, *where's this cat?*

I kept calling her, couldn't find her, and as I glanced out the window, I noticed something that looked like a tail flutter past the mirror.

I thought, *no way!* But sure enough, on the top of that A-frame was Buddy. She's hanging out with her front paws on the front post and her back paws on the back post, her tail fluttering in the wind.

By now, I'm doing like 35, 40 miles an hour, and I'm looking up at Buddy thinking, *what do I do?* Hit the brakes? I was afraid she was going to fall off, and I may run over her.

I rolled the window down, real slow, and I reached up through the A-frame, over top of her so she wouldn't jump, and I grabbed the back of her neck and yanked her into the truck.

She landed on the bunk and took off running all around. Then she looked at me and jumped up on the dash and looked out the window, like *I want to go back up there.*

And I sat there scolding her, telling her, "don't you ever do that again." And she just sat on my dash as I was pointing my finger at her, giving her a good lecture.

After that, I left my window open a couple of times and sat outside the truck, just to see if she would come out the window. But she never did that again.

And that's the story of Buddy the Trucker Kitty. She was one weird cat. She was also a good cat. And far too smart...for a cat.

Buddy eventually retired to my parent's farm and lived out a long kitty life.

PEOPLE IN MY TRUCK

Spending two weeks in a truck with another person, especially someone you don't know very well, can be trying. The quarters are very, very tight, and you're basically in each other's space every hour of the day, day after day.

Here are some of my stories.

I started my trucking career with Swift. After a while, I became a trainer for them and that's when things got interesting.

They'd shoot me a message, usually when I was coming into Green Bay, and say, "Hey, we got a student for you. He'll be here this afternoon."

I'd swing by, meet some guy, put him in my truck, and for the first day he would just sit in the passenger seat and watch as we drove off my hours. The next day, he would drive like four hours and then I'd drive the rest of my shift. After a week, the student was expected to drive a full shift, then I would drive my shift.

But, when you're with somebody whose driving skills are mostly untested, and you're expected to go in the back and sleep while this total stranger drives you down the road...things can get a little scary.

Once I woke up in a ditch. The student I was training couldn't really speak English. He was from Russia and he was a truck driver over there, but when he came to the United States, Swift made him go through the training program.

The guy knew how to drive a truck, but his lack of English was a problem.

Back then, Swift had a rule when a student was backing up, the trainer was not allowed to be inside the truck. He had to be outside the truck watching everything, guiding the student, telling him how to maneuver so no one got hit, and nothing got damaged.

While I was training for Swift, I always did this one run. It was a really tight schedule, and I would get very, very little sleep.

We would start heading down to Louisville, Kentucky, and I'd have the student drive from just below Gary on 65 down to Louisville, which is like four hours. When we'd get there, the student would wake me up and I'd help him back into the driveway and unload the truck.

Then we'd take off for the return trip and I'd go back to sleep while the student drove back to Gary. This would get me maybe six hours of sleep a day. After a few days, I'd be really tired.

I was on one of these trips with my Russian student, but he didn't wake me up when we got to the yard. He'd been there before, backed in there before, and must've thought, *you know what, I can do this.*

Next thing I know, I wake up to the whole truck just shaking like crazy, shimmying all over the place. And I'm like, *what in the world?*

I jump up, pull back the curtain, and while standing there in my underoos, I realize the whole truck is tipped in the air. I look over at the mirror next to him to see the drive tires about a foot and a half off the ground. Then the whole truck came down again, he'd catch traction and the truck would bounce back up in the air like a seesaw.

I yelled, "Stop!" He stopped. I popped the brakes and told him to put it in neutral. He did. Then I looked at him, unbuckled his seatbelt and said, "Get out of the truck right now."

He got out, walked across the road and sat down.

I pulled on some pants, then got out to assess the situation. Wheels up off the ground, the whole trailer was twisted, nearly tipped over in a ditch. I grabbed some blocks of wood, put them on the frame then dropped the airbags, which pushed the wheels back down. That gave me just enough traction to pull the trailer out of the ditch and keep it from tipping over completely.

I went over to have a chat with him, after I calmed down, and said, "You're not allowed to do that. You have to wake me up."

"I know. I just felt bad because you needed sleep." At least that's what I could pick out between the Russian.

"You still have to wake me up."

He became the best student I ever had.

I've also had some really weird guys in my truck.

There was this one guy, a really tiny guy with no chin.

We were driving down the road out in Nebraska, just flat, flat country. He was behind the wheel and out in the distance, a good half a mile, I saw what truckers call a gator, the tread off a blown tire, laying in the middle of the lane.

There was nothing else around, no cars, nothing but straight open country, and that long gator up ahead.

So, I sat there, watching him staring out the window driving right at the thing. We got closer and closer, and at the last second, I reached over and cranked the wheel.

We just missed it, the truck swerving everywhere.

He yelled, "What are you doing?"

I said, "Look in your mirror. You almost ran that over."

"Oh, I didn't see that."

I lost count of how many times I had to do that. Scared the Dickens out of me every time.

Come to find out, this guy had been kicked out of many trainers' trucks, which is why Swift asked me to try. They said I had the patience for it.

So, after I got this guy through the full training program plus two weeks extra, Swift called me up. "Well, is he gonna make it?"

I said, "Nope."

"Does he need another two weeks?"

"Nope. It is my belief, he'll never get it.

So, they pulled him out of my truck.

Then a week or two later, I was delivering at one of my places, and a student that I'd just trained came over and I was like, "Hey, how's it going?

He said, "I have a question. I got a guy in my truck. We're both going through our training part as students and the guy says you were his trainer."

And I'm like, *okay.*

"So, you passed this guy? You said he was good?"

"Who is it?"

We walked over to his truck, I looked up into the cab, turned around and said, "No. I told them he wasn't good."

The guy shrugged. "They told me he was the student I was to train with, so I came up here and met him. We've been driving. He's terrible."

Eventually, they gave the guy his own truck after spending several more months training him. They even built him a special seat that moved up far enough so he wouldn't need pillows and cushions to be comfortable.

A week later, he quit.

On the first day the guy got into my truck, I asked him about his experience, what school he'd attended, and he's like, "Well, I went to school with Schneider. I was going through their training program and they fired me."

That should have been my first clue. But I asked, "Why did they fire you?"

"Well, I went through the training program and they put me into a truck. I drove five miles down the road and got pulled over by the police who told me to sit and wait.

"And a few minutes later a little Schneider pickup truck arrived, the driver got out, told me to move over, and he drove me back to the yard."

"Why?" Figured I may as well know the rest.

"They said I drove off the driveway, put the trailer into the ditch, and then ran over a stop sign while I was leaving. They didn't want me there, so they called the police to find me and shut me down."

I think I was lucky to get out in one piece.

And then there are the couples.

A lot of people who come out here on the road bring their wife or girlfriend or maybe the woman drives and the guy rides along. It's actually better because it makes the time pass faster. It can also be a stressful thing too, 'cause it makes an already tight space, even tighter.

I tried it with my wife many, many, years ago.

She wanted to see the western part of the country, go out into the mountains and beyond. I'd been taking loads out that way and so I was like, "Okay, come ride with me."

She'd just been laid off from work and instead of sitting at home, she packed a bag and piled into my truck. And during that whole time, about three months I think, Swift never sent me west past the Mississippi. It was crazy. I asked them a few times, could you send me west, but they didn't have any freight going that way.

So, my wife was like, "I've seen this already. I don't want to be here."

But I didn't have any control over it.

Still, it was a good time and an eyeopener for her.

A lot of people say, "Oh, you're a truck driver. You get to see all kinds of interesting stuff…the beautiful countryside…the ocean."

Really what I get to see are the lines on the side of the road.

Yeah, you get glimpses of the sea, the mountains, and a few neat things. But it's not like I'm on vacation where I can stop and look at the different sites. Basically, I'm up and down the roads with a schedule to keep. I got to keep the truck moving.

Another eyeopener for my wife was how many hours I drove each day. That was stressful for her because she could not sleep when the truck was moving. She just couldn't do it. I mean, after days of her not sleeping, I'd get into a shipper, climb into the back for two or three hours or so, and by the time she would get all situated and fall asleep, I'd be unloaded and taking off again.

Another point of stress…I don't stop a lot. I don't eat multiple meals during the day. I've always done it that way. That was hard for her get used to. When we would stop, I'd hear her on the phone with her mom, "Oh my goodness, Larry's just given me a really good treat. We're actually gonna stop for a bit and I'm going to get a shower and get to do laundry and eat a meal!"

Then one day, she got really hungry. I carry food and stuff in the truck, but she got really hungry this one time and she asked, "Hey are we going to stop and grab something to eat, soon?"

So, I pulled off into a truck stop and we went in the Subway there. The person behind the counter asked, "Want a six inch or a foot long?"

My wife said, "Make it a foot long." Then she turned and looked at me, "But I'm not going to eat the whole thing. I'm going to save the other six inches. That way I have something for later."

And I was like, "I don't care."

So, we got our subs and stuff and took off driving. I'm woofing mine down and she's over there carefully working through hers. Then she wraps up the other six inches and sticks it down in her door.

I'm driving a few more minutes, and we're not really doing

anything, not talking, just looking out the window, when I hear paper crinkling.

I turn and look over at her and she's got her back to me, hunched over like, and I ask, "what's going on?"

She kind of pauses, I'm leaning forward trying to see what she's up to. Finally, I ask. "What are you doing?"

She turns slowly and looks at me. Her mouth is stuffed, her cheeks puffed out. "I'm hungry!"

"And you're trying to hide it from me?"

We both started laughing.

Sometimes it is a treat to have someone in your truck.

So, if you decide to become a truck driver and you end up going through a training program with a trainer, here's the best advice: Remember that truck is that trainer's home, treat it with respect, don't make demands. You are the visitor. If he turns out to be a complete tool, no big deal. Just call the company, ask for a new trainer and always keep moving forward.

SEE SOMETHING, SAY SOMETHING

It was a long time ago, back when I worked for Swift Transportation. I'd delivered a load to McDonough, Georgia, in the morning. I'd been running all night and was exhausted and needed a break, but the receiver of the cargo in my truck wouldn't let me park on their lot. My next load wasn't going to be ready until later that night, so I had plenty of time to take my break. I just needed a place to park.

I'd come up through the south side of McDonough. Let's just say it wasn't a good neighborhood. I drove up a narrow street and saw an abandoned factory warehouse. It had a small lot, and the building had busted-out windows and plenty of graffiti, but my choices were few. Besides, there were no cars around and no traffic on the street, so I figured nobody would bother me there.

I parked my truck in the lot, parallel to the street. A small gas station sat across from there. *Okay,* I thought. *I can find me something to eat at the gas station if I need to, and I'll be set, until my next load tonight.* It was a sunny spring day so I closed up the curtains of the Freightliner and got comfy in my Batman underoos—that's what most people call underwear—and crawled into bed to catch some much-needed shuteye.

Later on, around dusk, a commotion outside woke me. I got out of bed, sat in the driver's seat and peered through the curtains. Several police officers and a crowd of teenagers had collected across the street at the small gas station. It looked like the station was some type of hangout for a not-so-good-looking crowd. *Might be trouble*, I thought.

Several squad cars had their lights going. The officers tried to contain the angry crowd as the onlookers yelled, "Leave them alone!" Other colorful expressions were flung at the cops, who were having a heated discussion with two black teens in particular. As things escalated, about five more squad cars came in hot as back up.

'Course I'm just sitting there with my window down, leaning halfway out, enjoying the cool spring evening while chilling in my Batman underoos, watching what was like a live version of *Cops*. It was quite the show.

I noticed one of the teens getting really agitated. Wearing a white muscle tee and saggy pants, he looked about eighteen years old. Two officers were trying to detain his buddy, who weighed maybe ninety pounds soaking wet, but he sure was putting up a fight for such a little bean. White Shirt yelled and threatened the officers for trying to arrest his friend. Other cops were trying to talk the shouter down. The officers warned the eighteen-year-old to walk away or else he's "…gonna go downtown."

The cops weren't taking White Shirt too seriously. Periodically the cops would take a step toward him in an attempt to get him to back off and avoid going to jail himself. His pants had fallen halfway down his butt, and he was trying to act all tough, yet every time the cops yelled at him or took a few steps toward him, he'd run twenty or thirty feet into the street toward the warehouse, in order to get distance from the police, then turn around and start yelling at them again. It was pretty funny. The cops must have thought so, too, because they were laughing. The kid ended up backing up so far that he was about ten feet from my truck.

The commotion continued at the gas station parking lot as the crowd kept yelling at the police. Two officers ended up throwing Little Bean on the ground, and another officer actually had to sit on him to stop his squirming. They handcuffed him behind his back and cuffed his ankles, yet he was still going nuts and acting stupid. He wouldn't give up, just like his friend who was now across the street near my truck, watching.

Then I saw one of the officers do something that probably wasn't the nicest thing, although they were pretty tired of the situation. Half a dozen squad cars had shown up, and officers all over the place were trying to control the increasingly rowdy crowd. An imposing cop who looked like a professional body-builder took a pair of handcuffs that had a long chain between them and he used them to basically hog-tie Little Bean. Officer Imposing reached down and grabbed the chain, picked Little Bean up with one hand, yelled to another officer to open up a squad car door, and he just went *fwump*, and threw Little Bean onto the backseat.

Ohhh, boy, did that set off some people! 'Course White Shirt was still standing near my truck. Little Bean was his buddy, so throwing the kid into the squad car really set him off. He yelled and threatened the cops even more than he'd been doing.

Finally, one cop said to White Shirt, "That's it. I'm tired of you. You're gone," and two officers began walking toward the kid. They weren't taking him too seriously because they thought they were just dealing with a bunch of teens acting like punks.

White Shirt ran about fifty feet up the street, which led to a small residential section on the hill at the street's top. I could see the kid from my truck, but the officers couldn't. So I watched him for a while. He looked really nervous; I could tell he was deciding whether or not to take a stand. A few minutes later, he came back down the hill to the lot until he stood beside my truck.

From his new position, White Shirt started yelling at the cops like he had before. One officer again said, "That's it. You're done." I glanced down at the kid near my truck. This time he wasn't turning around and running away like he did before. He reached behind and under his white muscle-shirt and stuck his hand into his underwear. As I looked down at White Shirt, I thought, *Huh. This is a weird time to decide you need to scratch your butt.* Then I saw him reach farther into the back of his underwear and very slowly pull a gun out from behind his back.

Whooaah, I thought. I sat there assessing the situation. Three officers were walking toward White Shirt in order to detain him. To tell you the truth, they were not paying much attention to him. I think they thought he wasn't a threat, just a kid thinking he's a thug. No big deal. None of them saw him pull this gun out. Clearly, the kid was waiting for them to get closer so he could shoot the officers.

I sat there thinking hard. *What do I do?* When the officers were twenty-five feet away, I saw the kid put his thumb on the hammer and cock the gun. He was ready to shoot. All of a sudden I made the decision and said to myself, *This ain't cool.* And I yelled out, "*He's got a gun!*"

Then I rolled out of my seat, still in my underoos, and went down in between the seats as I heard a *pop-pop-pop-pop-pop-pop-pop!*

As the shots continued, I rolled out the passenger-side door and down the steps—still in my underwear, mind you—and landed on the ground on my hands and knees. From there I scampered down and hid behind the drive wheels, scrunched into a little ball, figuring the dual wheels would protect me.

The shooting finally stopped, but I stayed put. I had no clue what was going on or what to do, so I peeked from underneath my tandems, trying to see what happened. That's when I heard something behind me. I hesitantly turned around and saw a police officer walk around my truck with his gun drawn and pointing at me. He looked at me and started chuckling.

"Are you the truck driver?"

"Yeah...I'm the one who yelled 'He's got a gun'"

He holstered his weapon and said, "Thanks, dude. You just saved our lives. How about you get some clothes on?"

We both laughed.

I jumped up in the truck, threw on some clothes and glanced out the window. White Shirt lay in the road, he'd been shot. His gun lay beside him, and the other people in the parking lot were freaking out more than ever. Officers were everywhere and sirens were blaring. It was a wild sight.

I hopped back out of my truck and started looking around. There was a hole in the side of my hood that went clear through to the other side. I turned around and saw bullet holes all over the side of the abandoned warehouse.

Two police officers came over and talked to me for a while, asking me questions and taking my statement. As they did this, I noticed a guy standing beside a beat-up Cutlass near the pumps at the gas station across the street. The Cutlass had been lowered until it nearly hit the ground, and I could tell the guy who drove that vehicle was a bad dude—the rough kind.

Cutlass was giving the cops a hard time, yelling and hollering. A police officer had to hold him back as he looked at me talking to the cops.

Another cop walked across the street to my truck. He was Officer Imposing, the same officer who'd thrown Little Bean in the back of the squad car like a suitcase. He looked tense. "Hey, where are you heading?" he asked me.

I started to feel nervous. "I have a pick up about thirty miles north of here later tonight."

"You gotta leave, man. All right, this is what we're gonna do…"

Then I realized something I hadn't noticed before this. To be perfectly honest with you, I was probably the only white guy in that neighborhood aside from a few white police officers, and now I just snitched on White Shirt. The guys from the hood who stood in the gas station lot didn't like that, because they lived life as "them" versus the "police." It turned out the guy over by the Cutlass was a major gang boss in the area. The cops were worried he'd get my info off my truck and put a hit out on me.

"We got more squads on the way. As soon as the other cops get here, they're going to block all the side-streets. That dude with the Cutlass doesn't like you, man. We're gonna get you outta here."

I hopped into my truck, fired up the engine and looked at Officer Imposing.

"Go!" he yelled as he pointed to the road. I did a U-Turn and got the heck out of there. Boy, I could see Cutlass getting really hot and angry. He wanted to follow me and find me.

I took off out of town and ran up north about fifteen miles, then I doubled-back south, figuring anyone who might be coming after me would think I stopped off at the rest area on the north-bound side of the road. An officer followed me the whole way. We both pulled into the rest area north of town, and I shut off the motor. I hopped out of my truck and went to the squad car.

"Do you think this is good enough?"

"Yeah, this is good." He hesitated. "But, I'm just gonna wait here with you and keep an eye on you while you take your break. How long you gonna be here?"

"Well, I got about three hours until my next pickup." I showed him where I was headed.

"All right. I'll stay here, and then I'll follow you to the other place and hang out with you and follow you for about thirty minutes after you get loaded, just to make sure no one else is tracking you."

"Wow..."

"Yeah, this guy is not happy with you. We know who he is. We need to get you out of here safe and sound because, if he figures out who you are, he'll get somebody to take you out."

"Well, what about the guy who got shot?" I knew White Shirt was still alive, because he'd been moaning and groaning on the pavement when I left the scene.

"He's still alive. The paramedics are there. He's gonna make it."

"Okay, I was kinda worried about that. I didn't wanna cause his death, but I didn't want you guys to get shot either."

"Yeah, those police officers said to tell you 'thanks', man. You really saved their lives."

I returned to my truck for a few more hours. I tried to sleep, but the attempt proved pointless. Adrenaline raced through me, and I questioned the decision I'd made back at the lot across from the gas station. The sound of the gunshots echoed in my head. It's true I didn't want to see the cops get hurt, but I didn't want to see White Shirt get hurt either. To tell you the truth, I don't even know if he ever actually fired the gun.

The police contacted me about a week afterwards and said they needed me to come to McDonough and provide a formal state-ment, because White Shirt was claiming the gun was just lying in the road and wasn't his. The kid was just being stupid. The police needed me to contradict his claim. I agreed to help. But after three months of calling back and forth to the police department and the DA's office and never really getting anywhere, I finally called the police and asked about the status of the case, and if they still needed me.

"Yeah, you don't actually need to come down anymore."

"Oh, did he plead guilty or something?" I asked.

"No, he's dead."

"*What*? He died from that?"

"Oh, no! He got shot again. We took him to the hospital that night and got him fixed up. But we released him, and a week and half later he was killed in a gang shooting."

So that's my big story! I was in the middle of a gun battle down in McDonough, Georgia—in my underoos, no less. Rolling down the road, I still think about that incident sometimes. I still don't know why they released the kid. For a while there I felt guilty, like I was responsible for getting him killed. But he made his choice, and I made mine.

If you see something, say something, and stick to your choices when you know it's the right thing to do.

FROM CONE CLIPPING TO WEDDING BELLS

Before I tell this story, I just have to say this was many years ago, and the statute of limitations has come and gone.

I was working for Swift Transportation, and a buddy of mine—who went through training school with me—worked for Swift too. Sometimes they'd put us on the same runs, and we'd get to drive together, kind of like a convoy.

So, we were driving—I think it was in Wyoming or Colorado—and it was the middle of the night.

I was out in front, there were no cars around, and we were going through this single-lane construction zone, talking back and forth over the CB.

Bored, I said, "You know what? I bet you I can launch an orange barrel farther than you can."

He came back, "Well, let's see one."

Coming up on one of those orange barrels, I gave my steering wheel a quick jerk, swung my trailer out a little bit, and clipped the barrel with my trailer tires. It hit hard, and the barrel just flew through the air.

My buddy came back on the radio, laughing and laughing. "Man, that thing flew pretty good. Let me try."

So, there we were, driving through this single-lane construction zone clipping orange barrels here and there, just having a good time.

The construction zone ended, and some miles later, we came to a scale. It was open.

So I drove up onto the scale, and a guy came over the loud-speaker and said, "pull around back."

I keyed my CB mic and said, "Dude, they're pulling me in."

"Awwww, man!"

I pulled off the scale and was driving around back when my buddy came over the CB again, "Dude, they're pulling me in too."

So there we were, parking our trucks, and the Scale Master is walking toward us.

We got out of our trucks and asked, "What's up?" I knew we weren't overweight, but he looked serious.

"Were you guys having some fun back in the construction zone?"

My buddy and I just looked at each other. Our careers were on the line.

"Were you hitting orange barrels on purpose?"

We both shrugged, and he kept talking. "We got a call that there were two semis, two Swift drivers, going through the construction zone hitting barrels."

"Who would do that?" my buddy asked.

The guy motioned us toward my buddy's truck. "Come here."

We followed him around the back of my buddy's cab, and he pointed at the empty space between the cab of the truck and the trailer and asked, "What's that?"

We both leaned in, and there it was...an orange barrel stuck in between the truck and the trailer.

We started talking at the same time, but the Station Master interrupted. "I get it. It's the middle of the night. You guys are bored. But you can't be doing that."

How hard was the ax going to fall?

The man kept talking. "Now, I'll tell you what you're gonna do. You're gonna pull that barrel out of there, you're going to stick it over by that dumpster. Then you're going to get back in your trucks and get outta here. And you're gonna stop acting like idiots."

We started yanking on that barrel like crazy. It was really wedged up in there, but we pulled it free and got out of there.

Then we started laughing again.

Driving together was a good time for him and me.

He actually met his wife while out on the road.

We were in a diner down in Illinois at a truck stop, and there was this attractive waitress.

Now, I'm always talkative, nice to everybody, and I was talking to her. I wasn't married at the time. I was dating someone, but we weren't married yet, and I wasn't really hitting on her, just talking to her.

She laughed, walked away, and my buddy asked, "What are you doing? You've got a girlfriend."

"I'm just talking to her. What...do you like her or something?"

"She is pretty hot."

She came back to our table, and I started talking to her again and introduced her to my buddy. "He's an awfully nice guy. You know what you should do?"

She asked, "What's that?"

"You should let my buddy take you out."

She turned, looked at him. "Well, is your buddy going to ask me?

I looked at my buddy. He was just sitting there. So I kicked him under the table, and he looked up at me, then at her.

"Are you going to ask me?" she said again.

He did, and they saw each other every time he was down that way.

It was a couple months later he quit Swift for a local job, I asked him what was going to happen with his girl. "You won't get down that way driving local."

"Oh, she's moving out here with me."

And she did. Then they married and are still married today.

Kinda neat, isn't it?

TURKEY ONE, MACK TRUCK ZERO

I was working for Schwinn Trucking as a mechanic, and it was the day before Thanksgiving.

A driver called in sick, so the guy who did scheduling for the trucks asked me if I could cover things for the night. I said "sure" and jumped into a '68 or '69 Mack Cruiseliner cabover. It had chrome Texas bumpers, a flat front with a big square grill, and a big ol' Mack bulldog ornament between the top of the grill and the bottom of the windshield that stuck straight out several inches. If you've ever seen the *BJ and the Bear* TV show, you know exactly the kind of truck I'm talking about.

Anyway, my wife at the time, worked for Schwinn, too. She was about to go home for the day but changed her mind and said, "Well, I'll just ride with you for the night."

So, she came with me, and we went on our first of three or four runs, picking up tankers of liquid whey from Baker Cheese and taking them to Milk Specialties in Adell on 57, south of Plymouth.

It was about a 40-mile trip, and we'd be running back and forth all night. But I grew up out there, so I kind of knew the back roads, so that made it easier.

The tanker was a food-grade tanker. Food tankers don't have baffles in them, and they can only fill them like three-quarters full, which puts them at max weight. So, if you ever have to hit the brakes or something like that, while hauling one of these, and that liquid starts to slosh, it can push you around really bad.

So, I was loaded, running along on this back road, County U it was. There's a prison there. And right around that prison, there are a lot of animals. A lot of deer, a lot of turkeys, all kinds of critters. Nobody can hunt back around the prison, so nothing ever gets thinned out. There's quite a variety of wildlife.

It was just starting to get a dark out, and we'd just gone past the prison, maybe a couple hundred feet, when I saw a turkey jump out up ahead of me and I was like, "Oh my."

Turkeys are all muscle and can mess up a truck really bad if you hit one.

My wife looked up as another turkey jumped out, then another turkey jumped out, then another and another. A whole line of them were running up out of a ditch and trying to cross the road. There must've been five or more.

I was kinda timing things and stuff, steered over onto the other side of the road to get behind them, they were running across, and I thought, *I'm just going to miss them.* When the fifth

Turkey got to the middle of the road, I would drive right behind him. It was all going to be good.

Then one little straggler decided he needed to cross, too.

He jumped outta the ditch, looked at me and was like, *Whoa!* And instead of following his buddies, that bird turned and ran away from me, straight up the middle of the road. There was just nothing I could do. I was applying the brakes, but I knew I couldn't stomp on them. Not with a loaded food-grade tanker behind me.

So, this turkey is running and running and running for his dear life, and the truck is gaining and gaining on him, and then just before I reached it, that turkey took off. It flew.

Turkeys really don't fly very well or far. They mostly kind of glide. They'll kind of take off, get a little bit of air, but then...

Wham!

And I was like, *ouch.*

So, I'm looking in my mirrors, back both sides, expecting feathers and everything else to be flying. I figured he hit my Texas bumper.

But, there was nothing.

I said to my wife, "Where'd it come out? Did you see it come out?"

Then I heard this noise, and I was like, "what in the heck is that?"

She kept looking, and I leaned forward to try and see down toward the grill and there it was.

That turkey was stuck on the chrome bulldog. It was flapping its wings like there was no tomorrow, trying to fly while I'm still driving down the road.

I started laughing and my wife, she started screaming as the bird kept getting higher and higher, closer and closer to the windshield, wings flapping like crazy, that bulldog basically right up his butt.

I'm still laughing, she's screaming, I kind of tapped the brakes, and the bird flew off, went about a foot or so and glided into another ditch.

I kept going and when we got down to Adell, I looked at the front of the truck. The whole grill was bent into a "U" shape. It was really bad. But turkeys are like 15 to 20 pounds and pretty much all muscle. They are really tough.

And there were feathers and more stuck in the grill. So, I pulled the feathers out, then pulled on the grill a little bit trying to straighten it. They're basically fake, but I didn't want to pull it off the front end of the truck. So, I kind of left it as it was, finished the runs and drove back to the yard.

But before I did, I went back past the prison, pulled over right at the spot, and with a flashlight looked through the ditches. I thought for sure that turkey would be laying in one of them. It'd be a waste to not grab it and take it home. It was Thanksgiving, after all.

But I couldn't find that turkey anywhere. He was one tough bird.

So, with the runs finished, and the truck returned, I figured I'd come in early and fix the grill. But before I left, I stuck all the feathers from the grill in the little cup holder thing between the seats.

The next day, I arrived early, and the boss's brother, who was the day mechanic, already had the grill all ripped off. It was on the shop floor and he was jumping on it, try to bend it back.

I'm like, "Oh, you're fixing that?"

"Yeah, Boss wants me to fix it quick cause there's a driver showing up in a minute who needs his truck."

I jumped up into the cab to grab my feathers, the guy yelled, "What'd you hit? A turkey?"

I looked out at him through the windshield and yelled back, "How would you know that?" Then I looked down into the cupholder. "Hey, where's my feathers?

The boss, who must have heard us talking, came out of his office. "That's my truck. Them's my feathers."

We laughed and I asked, "So, what are you gonna do with the feathers?"

"I'm stickin' 'em on my wall as payment from the turkey who bent my grill."

CLOSE CALL

I was driving for Swift, running back and forth across Missouri. Back then, the Swift trucks were governed at 60 miles per hour. Now I think they're closer to 65, or maybe even 67.

Anyway, it was about four o'clock in the morning and I was cruising along at 60 miles per hour, sharing the road with this heavy-haul guy pulling a big piece of machinery on a lowboy trailer. It was one of those trailers that drop in the front so they can easily drive bulldozers or whatever right off. They're pretty cool.

The road was three lanes across, with very little traffic, and this guy was constantly coming up alongside me, trying to pass.

But, every time he'd get beside me, we'd be nearing a hill. He'd bog down and I kept going.

Well, he tried this about six or seven times and every time an incline forced him to fall back.

Some drivers, when trying to pass, get all frustrated and end up cutting you off, or worse. So, I decided, the next time he came alongside me, I was just going to slow down and let the guy go.

It wasn't long before he was back, trying again. I kicked my cruise control off, slowed the truck down, and let the guy pass. Eventually, he got in front of me.

By now, the sun was starting to peek over the horizon, traffic was picking up and I got a good look at the piece of equipment on his trailer. It was a giant excavator with a huge arm that extended out over the trailer's back end. But there was no bucket, or anything attached. Instead, the arm ended in a long spike.

And that big old spike was just hanging out there, pointing straight down.

Anyway, the guy was probably a hundred yards or so up ahead of me. We were climbing another slight hill and the road was getting a little rough when all of a sudden I saw his taillights start bouncing, really bad.

Then the sky lit up. I mean, it was instant. Like the sun was suddenly burning right in front of me.

I stood on the brakes knowing I had to be flying up on this guy who must be braking, too. And then I saw it. The excavator's giant boom had bounced off the trailer and that big ol' spike was now sticking straight into the asphalt. It stopped the guy on a dime.

His trailer was sideways across traffic, the excavator pulled off to the side of it, and his truck spanned the whole road.

I had a split second to make a life or death decision.

Still standing on the brakes, I knew I'd never stop in time.

I grabbed the airbrake and decided to put my truck into a jack-knife. There was a concrete wall to my right and nobody between it and me, so I swung toward it, bypassed the ABS, and locked up the trailer brakes

My trailer started to slide out and my bumper was just *boom, boom, boom,* hitting that concrete wall, which was helping me slow down. But it still wasn't gonna be enough.

Then I remembered, "look where you want to go." It was a favorite saying of an instructor at the Fox Valley Technical College where I attended. A ditch, just past the guy's truck caught my eye and I aimed for it.

It's amazing how focusing on where you want to go, instead of the turmoil happening around you, opens up opportunity.

Heading for the ditch, my truck finally stopped right at the edge and I actually closed my eyes, certain somebody was going to plow into me. The sounds of squealing tires was everywhere.

When all was quiet, I opened my eyes and looked out my mirror. Cars were all over the road, one with its hood stuck underneath my trailer. The guy's truck was just a few yards ahead of mine, his lowboy right next to me. I opened my driver's side door and stepped right on to his trailer.

I got out and just stood there, legs shaking.

The guy hauling the excavator came running up to me and said,

"I can't believe you didn't hit me. All I could think of is you coming right up over the flatbed and plowing through me. I jumped out of my truck and took off running."

I was like, "yeah."

It was time for a fresh pair of underoos.

WHY MY HEAD RATTLES

This isn't exactly trucking related. But I get a lot of comments from viewers on my YouTube Channel who say "You're crazy. You make all these funny sounds and voices. What's up with that?"

Well, here're some stories that might help you understand.

If you ever get the chance to ask my father, "What's up with Larry?" he'll tell you two things.

First, he'll say "Oh that Larry, he can fix anything."

Then he'll add, "and he's been trying to kill himself since he was born."

It's true. I've had some pretty good whopping accidents. Some were my fault. Some were other people's fault because they were the ones in charge of me.

Anyway, when I was five or six years old, we had a big working farm. I can't remember how many cows we milked, but it was quite a few. And we had about a hundred pigs, and lots of chickens, too.

When it came time to milk, which happened every day in the early morning and then again in the evening, the whole family worked to get everything done. My dad had a full-time job, so my mom was kind of in charge of the farm's daily workings, but dad always helped out on the weekends when he was home.

We milked the cows in the barn. Above the barn, in the loft, was the hay we used to keep the cows quiet during the milking. My next older brother and I had the job of climbing into the loft and dropping bales down through holes in the floor where they'd land in front of the metal stanchions we used to hold the cows in place.

Then we'd go down and break the bales into pads, place the cows into the stanchions, and give each a pad of hay to eat while they were being milked. It kept the cows happy and occupied, and they didn't try to kick the milk bucket.

So, it was early one Sunday morning. My brother and I were in the loft, and he started opening the doors that covered the holes through the floor. They had these big metal rings on them, and the openings were just a little bigger than the bales.

I pulled a bale to the floor and then started pushing it toward one of the holes. The hay bale weighed more than I did. I was just a skinny little kid. My brother would always try to help me, but I'd push him away, wanting to do it on my own.

I finally got the hay bale to the edge of the hole, gave it one last shove, and this time I went with it through the hole, my hand stuck in the binding twine.

So, I'm falling about ten feet through the hole, hit the barn's stone and mortar foundation, and then I bounced off and hit the concrete floor, headfirst.

My mom was there, setting up for the milking, and saw the whole thing happen. I don't exactly remember what I did next, but this is how my mom tells the story.

After bouncing off the foundation wall with my head and shoulders, which slowed me down a little bit, and then the top of my head smacking straight down on the concrete floor, I was knocked unconscious. Completely gone. So, she took me into the house and had my sister stay with me. She needed to get back to the barn because you can't just stop milking.

My sister held ice on my head, made sure I kept breathing, and watched for me to wake up.

Sometime before the milking was finished, I came to. My sister went to get our mom and told her, "Larry's awake, but he doesn't seem right."

My mom came in, checked me over, and kept asking me if I was okay, and I was like, "my head hurts." Then I'd say, "who are you?"

So, they finished the milking and kept messing with me, and since it was Sunday, everybody got ready to go to church. My mom was like, "I don't think Larry's going to church." So, she sat with me and everybody else left.

I stayed on a couch, looking straight up, my head all iced—and I do remember this, which is when it all started—the ceiling above me all of a sudden started moving farther and farther away. It was the weirdest thing.

My mom kept asking me questions—I don't remember if I said anything—and she said, "yeah, you got to go to the hospital." So, she brought the farm truck around, loaded me up and headed to the Emergency Room.

On the way there, every time she would look at me, I'd press myself harder into the passenger-side door, like I was scared and trying to get as far away from her as possible. Then I'd ask, "Who are you?"

We went into the Emergency Room, and, well, medical treatment back then wasn't like it is now. Nowadays you go to the hospital after a fall and you can be in there for three days just for tests amounting to $100,000. But the doctor looked me over and said, "well, he's got a concussion. Keep using the ice bags, aspirin, and keep him awake for as long as you can."

After that, my family wouldn't let me go outside for days. They wouldn't let me help or do anything.

And that's when my mechanical talents first kicked in.

They would all go outside, doing milking and things, and I was stuck inside, alone. Every once in a while, somebody would come in and check on me, making sure I was still okay.

One day, I was in the house messing around, and all of a sudden my mom came in to check on me. She walked through the entry hall and paused at the now doorless frame. Then she entered the family room. Again, no door.

It was an old farmhouse, nearly very interior room had a heavy-duty door of solid wood.

Then she walked into the living room, which was also minus its doors, and found me. I had taken off all hinges, removed all the doorknobs, and I had everything laid out on the coffee table in front of me. And she just stood there watching me examining each piece as if trying to figure out how each one worked with the others as she wondered how I'd removed half-a-dozen doors that each weighed more than me.

Finally, she spoke, and I do remember this clearly. She said, "When I get back, these doors," she pointed at each one scattered around the room, "better be put back together." Then she walked out of the house.

So, I put all the doors back together and got them back on their hinges, and I did it all with a butter knife and by using leverage underneath to put them back on the frames.

When my dad walked into the house—mom had told him what I was doing—he tried each rehung door. All the doors worked as good or better than before. He said to my mom, "are you sure about this?"

She said, "I swear the doors were off!"

That was my first major accident. And the thing where I lay down and look up at the ceiling and it starts to move farther and farther away from me, it still happens sometimes.

But the really weird stuff didn't start until I was about twelve.

It was my first year of deer hunting. My dad gave me an old pump 12-gauge shotgun and boy did that thing have a kick to it. I was still a runt of a kid and it could knock me flat.

My oldest brother was the one in charge of hunting, so he took me up to our spot a little before hunting season to put up a tree stand for me. Together, we found this tree that had a limb about two and a half to three feet off the ground, and then about fifteen degrees around the tree was another limb about two or three feet higher. And then there was another limb back the other way. It was almost like a ladder of limbs going up.

My brother crawled up in the tree and made sure he could see his tree stand from there so he could keep an eye on me when the season started. But it couldn't be too close. You don't want two hunters shooting at the same deer.

So, we built me a stand up in this tree, probably thirty-five to forty feet off the ground.

Opening morning of deer hunting rolled around, my brother led me and my old pump 12-gauge shotgun back to the tree and said, "Get up in the stand, sit as quietly as you possibly can. Wait for the light. As soon as the light comes out, you're going to start seeing stuff, fox, squirrels. Stay quiet. And if you see anything with horns, shoot it."

I'm like, "alright."

So, I climb the tree, got in the stand, the sun comes up, and I'm bored out of my mind! Standing up, I discovered if I craned my neck a certain way, I could just get a glimpse of my brother sitting in his tree stand.

I didn't want him to see me messing around, 'cause he'd get all upset with me, so I sat back down and stared up at the branch right above the stand, about six feet up. Resting my shotgun against the tree, I jumped on a nearby lower branch, then grabbed the higher branch and started doing pull-ups.

If I went way up, I could catch a better glimpse of my brother sitting rock-still. Then I saw a deer. It was walking right between my brother and me.

Well, I got all excited, dropped to the floor of the tree stand and grabbed my gun as fast as I could. The deer started running, probably from the noise of me hitting the boards, and I quickly swung out my gun, tracked the deer, and as soon as it got even close to being lined up, I pulled the trigger.

But I'd forgotten to plant my feet firmly, and as soon as I pulled that trigger, it gave me a big old wallop on my shoulder sending me backwards out of the tree stand.

And those branches that made it so easy to get up there, well they weren't fun going the other way. I hit the first branch with the back of my head, and it spun me around and face-planted me into the next one, which spun me back the other way and the next branch caught the back of my head, again. It was like being that round disk dropping thorough the big Plinko gameboard on The Price is Right.

Finally, I hit the ground. My face was killing me. It felt like a thousand needles were poking into my skin. Blood was everywhere.

Not far from me was my gun, the barrel stuck straight into the ground.

I pulled myself up, walked over to my gun and pulled it out of the muck. The barrel was packed full of mud.

I knew I needed to go look for the deer I just shot, and if it wasn't dead, I'd need to shoot it again, which meant I needed to clear the barrel. So, I grabbed a stick and went to work.

Then I heard a bunch of commotion coming through the brush behind me. I thought it was the deer running at me. So, I'm working faster, mud flying, and just when I expected the deer to burst through the brush, I aim the gun and it was my brother running straight at me.

"Whoa! Whoa!" he yelled, hands raised.

I lowered the gun. "Hey, did you see a deer over there?"

He stepped closer, just looking at me. Then he started laughing.

"What? What's so funny?"

He said, "Your face is so messed up."

I could feel my lips growing, each one about the size of a life-saver package. The skin was all split, blood oozing. My nose was busted and tipped over to the side. "I shot a deer over there."

"I didn't see no deer."

"Well, let's go look for it."

We walked over and looked around, but there was no blood. I probably didn't get within twenty feet of it. So, I said, "set my nose." I'd seen my father set his own nose a couple of times.

"Oh no. I'm not doing that because if I mess something up, Mom'll kill me. You need to go to the hospital."

I said, "look, if you take me home, mom's going to freak out and this'll be my last year hunting."

"I'll get you fixed up."

So, we headed for the emergency room.

When we got there, they wanted my parent's phone numbers, and my brother handed them over.

Soon my mom was running into the waiting room.

They took me back to an area divided by privacy curtains and assigned me a bed. I could hear my mom and brother arguing and finally, she came in to talk to me. While I was explaining what happened, telling her it was all my fault, a big commotion started outside the room. Seems another boy had been brought in, and there was a bunch of people working on him. It was hard not to get impatient. I was pretty busted up.

Then everything got quiet for the longest time until a nurse came into my area to check on me and explained that the doctor would be in soon. I asked, "What happened out there?"

"You fell out of a tree stand, right?" she asked quietly.

I nodded.

"Well, that was a twelve-year-old boy from Rosendale. He was deer hunting, too, and fell out of his tree stand, and he just passed away."

Four years passed before my next accident.

I was nearly sixteen years old, had saved and saved every penny I could put my hands on, and had finally bought my first car. It was an Opel, and it was a piece of junk. My plan was to fix it up so the moment I got my license, I'd have a car to drive.

There was a lot wrong with that car, but the worst part was the frame underneath the driver's seat was all rusted. But I had a plan and a welder. A little reinforcement and it'd be good.

Well, I found some old broken plowshares, which were basically the same width as the frame and grabbed my welder. The plan seemed perfect except that the frame was rusted mild steel and the plowshares were hardened spring-steel. The two do not weld together so good. I did the best I could and basically ended up with a bunch of booger welds. But it didn't need to look good.

By the time my sixteenth birthday arrived, I'd saved enough for insurance and registration. So, I asked my parents if I could go to the lake to hang with my buddies and water-ski. My mom was like, "Oh, you can't take your car, you don't have insurance on it.

I said, "Here's the money. Can you stop on your way to town and get me my insurance?"

She agreed and I headed to the lake in my very own car.

At the lake, another friend of mine, who lived on a really big farm, was there. It was supposed to rain the following day and his dad had sent him over to find anybody who wanted to make some money getting their hay in before the weather moved in. "My dad said he'd pay top dollar."

I'd just handed my parents my last dime, so I said, "I'm coming!" and jumped in my Opel.

Speeding down a narrow road to my friend's farm, I was going fast around a sharp bend. And as I came around that bend, an old dump truck was in my lane, coming right at me.

I tried to go to his left, to go around him, but he was trying to make a wide left turn into his driveway.

By the time I realized this and hit the brakes, I left about a ten-foot skid mark before hitting him so hard I broke the dump truck's axel and pushed it into the ditch.

The resulting impact folded my car into an "A" shape, the point of the "A" right beneath my seat where I'd welded the rusty frame. My legs and knees were on one side and the rest of me on the other, the folded floor pushing my right leg through the dash. My knee was busted open, and my leg and foot broken in multiple places.

Of course, I didn't have a seatbelt on. So, my chin hit the top of the steering wheel with such force that it pushed my jaw upward completely cracking my skull from the left side to my right ear. The top of my head also hit the windshield, breaking out the glass which was now laying on the hood.

The guy driving the dump truck, and his wife, said they came over and checked on me, but couldn't find a pulse. So, they went up to their house, grabbed the phone and called the police.

Here's what I remember. I was walking up to a house that had a bunch of beads hanging down in a doorway to a garage. I walked into the garage and pounded on the door to the house. The people in the house were on the phone telling someone what happened, telling them I was dead. The man kept talking on the phone and the woman answered the door. When she saw me, she screamed, passed out, and fell to the floor.

I just stepped over her toward the guy, took the phone out of his hand and hung up the receiver.

The guy ran over to his wife while I dialed my house.

Meanwhile, my mother was in town shopping and she got this really weird feeling that something was wrong, and she needed to go home. So, she left the store and drove the 20 miles back home. Now, my mom didn't go to town unless it was absolutely necessary because it cost money to get there. And when she was in town, she did as much as she possibly could.

The phone was ringing when she walked in the door. She picked up the receiver and it was me. I said, "I've been in an accident. I'll meet you at the hospital." Then I passed out and hit the floor.

I woke up in the emergency room and could hear my mom talking with the doctor. I was in the same big room, in what seemed like the same bed, with the same dividing curtains. And, once again, I started hearing a bunch of commotion going on. When my mom walked in, I asked, "What's going on out there?"

"They're working on another boy."

Doctors and nurses continued calling to each other, shouting for things I didn't understand. Monitors beeped and screamed. Hurried footsteps screeched on the waxed floors.

Then everything suddenly went quiet. In a little while, a nurse came in to check on me and assure my mom that the doctor would be in shortly.

I asked, "What's going on out there?"

"There was a boy out there, same age as you. He hit a truck head-on and just passed away."

That was twice in one lifetime.

After multiple surgeries and months of recovery spent watching The Beverly Hillbillies, Green Acres, Hogan's Heroes, Gilligan's Island and Happy Days, I visited my folded-up Opel and went back to where the accident happened.

You could see where my right leg went up into the dash. The seat was just inches from the broken steering wheel, and the door didn't open. No one could figure out how I got out of that car—including me. I have no recollection of pulling myself free or how I managed to walk on a broken leg with a busted knee and a fractured foot, the 100 yards or so up to the dump truck owners' house to use their phone.

Some might say I'm just hard-headed like that.

Some might agree that I've had it in for myself since my first birthday.

Or, perhaps that thing with the ceiling moving farther and farther away is actually a really big guardian angel making sure I'm around to deliver that one last load and fix that one more thing that needs fix'n (or taken apart).

So if you think I act a little strange at times, just remember that my brains probably rattle in my head.

THE SUCK-UP

At a shop where I worked as a mechanic early in my career, there was this one guy, he had a nickname, we'll say it was Wizzer, but it actually wasn't, it was kind of a naughty name. This was my boss's go-to guy. Wizzer would do anything my boss asked him and had his head shoved up my boss's butt so far it wasn't funny.

My boss's company had many divisions. One did a lot of wey hauling—milk and stuff like that. Another division of his company did municipal waste hauling.

People don't think too much about where waste goes when they flush their toilet. In big cities they have large waste treatment plants where it's processed completely. But smaller municipalities need help disposing of the residual sludge.

After the clean water is removed, the sludge remains. The sludge is hauled out of the treatment plants and spread on farm fields for fertilizer. The farmers are more than willing to take free fertilizer.

My boss had a whole division that went around to smaller municipalities, cities of 1,000-3000 people. They'd have two, maybe three settling ponds.

We'd come in, once or twice a year, with big vacuum machines, and suck all the sludge out of the bottom of the settling ponds, put it in tankers, and haul it out to farm fields.

We had huge tractors with big liquid manure spreaders. The big tines on the back would dig down in the ground and inject the sludge into the ground. It was great fertilizer for farmers. They couldn't grow crops for human consumption but could grow corn or wheat for cow feed.

We'd set up a job site and stay for a month or two to clean out one place. Trucks needed to come and go, turn the pumps on, load, run out to the farmer's field, and then we needed guys for the tractors. It was quite an involved process.

Sometimes in the first pond, the drains would get plugged up. We'd go in and find the drain and unplug it so the liquid would drain into the second pond.

One time we went to a place in Marshfield; my boss, Wizzer, and I. We'd always carry a rowboat with us so we could go out in the pond to move the pump nozzle around.

As often happened, the drain was plugged.

We had a blueprint of the pond showing us about where the drain was, a poured concrete drain with big metal bars across it. We'd grab a piece of pipe about 20 feet long, row our boat out to where the drain should be, and push the pipe down to the bottom until we hit concrete or the grate.

Once we found it, we'd move the pipe around and knock debris off so it would start draining. When you got a release like that, it was like a toilet bowl flush; the water started swirling around, then you'd have to row like crazy back to shore.

On this particular occasion, my boss, Wizzer, and I were out in the rowboat; I was in the bow, my boss was in the back, and Wizzer was rowing in the middle. We took turns with the pipe, searching and searching for hours; it was getting aggravating.

Ol' Wizzer got so frustrated that he offered to jump in and find it. My boss, thinking Wizzer was joking, said, "Yeah, go ahead if you want." While my boss and I sat there slack-jawed, Wizzer stood, ripped his shirt off, and dove into the sewage pond.

What just happened?

All of a sudden, Wizzer surfaced right by the boat, surprising my boss and me. He pulled himself up so his head was just above the side of the boat and growled, "Hand me the pipe!"

We both looked at him and started laughing hysterically at the same time. He was looking at us, asking, "What? What?"

I said, "Dude, there's a tampon sitting on top of your head."

Unfazed, he flicked it off, saying, "Whatever, give me that pipe."

I told my boss, "You can't let him stay there. If he's got any cuts or anything, he's going to get infected. He's going to get some kind of disease."

He said, "I didn't tell him to go in there."

I told him, "I know you didn't, you were just joking around, but I want to pull him out."

Then Wizzer started yelling that he found it. So we rowed over by him. He stuck the pipe into the hole, so I grabbed the top of it and moved it around. I said, "Yeah, it's stuck in there," and you could feel it was down inside the grate.

My boss asked if it would stay there by itself, and I said, "Yeah, it's stuck in there good. It'll stay right there."

We didn't want to open the drain and risk flushing Wizzer into the next pond.

Wizzer said, "All right, I'm coming in." He started grabbing the boat.

My boss put his hand in front of Wizzer and said, "Oh no, you're not."

Wizzer asked, "What?"

My boss said, "You just hang on to the front of the boat." He grabbed the oars and said, "I'll row over to the shore while you hang on. You're not flipping his boat with me in it!"

My boss liked to wash his equipment on site so we had a trailer-mounted pressure washer with a 500 gallon tank.

As we got near shore there were people watching what was going on; they couldn't believe it either. We got Wizzer to shore and my boss yelled for somebody to fire up the pressure washer and hose Wizzer off.

Poor ol' Wizzer had to stand while this guy pelted him head to toe with the pressure washer. It was so funny.

Yeah, he was my boss's boy and he would do anything he wanted.

It was crazy. There were some wild times at that place.

THE FIRST HYBRID CAB OVER

I was driving a 1968 Mack cab over truck, headed up to Clover, Wisconsin. There was a load that needed to go out but the driver got hung up during the day and wasn't going to be able to make the delivery, so they called me up from the shop where I worked maintenance at the time.

They said, "Hey, could you jump in a truck? Go pick up this load at Chilton and haul it to Clover and come back.?"

I said yeah, no problem, I'd go. So I jumped into the truck, went and got loaded, and ran up to Clover.

I ended up having to sit there all night long because the load was late. So I ended up sleeping there, and they got me unloaded in the morning.

I finally took off and was running back. I had let the truck run 'cause it was wintertime, so I was low on fuel and watching my fuel gauge intently. The Boss didn't have any fuel stops planned, everything he did was local and he had his own fuel tanks right at his shop.

I was running back towards Fond du Lac, the shop was about 15 miles east of there. I was watching my fuel gauge, thinking, *"I don't know if I'm going to make this or not."*

I kept watching my fuel gauge, and it was all the way on E from Oshkosh to Fond du Lac, which is about 15 miles. I knew I had to go all the way through town with stop and go traffic and climb a big hill out of Fond du Lac. I'd have hated to run out of fuel in the middle of the town. So I decided to stop at the Stretch Truck Stop just outside Fond du Lac, Wisconsin.

I was coming up to the exit, and as soon as I turned off, I started slowing down and pulled it out of gear to downshift. When I did, I noticed my fuel gauge drop all the way to zero. The engine died.

I laid off the brake and cruised pretty well. I was rolling up the off-ramp, looking back and forth on the road that I was going to cross. I didn't see any cars coming, so I just kept the truck rolling, made a left-hand turn, and crossed over the highway. The bridge over the highway had kind of a hump to it and I had just enough speed to roll over the top.

From the middle of the bridge, it was all downhill to the Stretch Truck Stop. I made it over and thought, *"I'm going to make this."* So I came down off of that overpass. Then there's an intersection with a right turn lane. No cars were coming, so I just went on through, made my right-hand turn, into the driveway to the truck stop; the pumps were straight ahead.

Three guys were walking across my path, I think they were

truck drivers leaving the truck stop diner. Usually I would have stopped to let them go. But if I would've stopped, I would have been sitting in the middle of the parking lot and not by the fuel pump where I needed to be.

I just kept going. One of the guys saw me coming, stopped, and kind of put his hand out. He must've said something to the other guys, and they both stopped, so I rolled right on past these guys and right up to the fuel pump. It was perfect. I thought, *"Wow, that couldn't have gone any better."*

I got out of the truck and grabbed the fuel nozzle, and started fueling, just wanting to put fifty bucks in the tank.

I looked up and the three guys were walking back towards me. I figured they're going yell at me 'cause I didn't stop or something.

The one guy comes walking up to me with a confused look on his face. He asked, "Why did you shut your truck off when you pulled in here?"

I turned and looked at him, without even thinking about it whatsoever, I said, "This is a hybrid."

He asked, "What?"

I said, "Yeah, this is a hybrid truck. You know what a hybrid is, right? It runs off electricity and fuel."

And he looked at me uncertainly and said, "What?"

I said, "Yeah, this is a test truck. Haven't you heard there might be new hybrid trucks coming?"

The guy was like, "Oh, I heard talk about hybrid trucks."

I told him, "Well, this is one of the test trucks they're doing it in. I was running off electricity when I came in."

The two guys that were standing behind him, they were looking at me. I could see the looks on their faces, they didn't believe a single word I was saying. But the guy I was talking to, he was just eating this up.

He asks, "Why did they put it in such an old truck?"

This was in 2006 or 2007 or something, and this was a 1968 truck—the guy I drove for took very good care of his trucks. He would always have custom paint jobs on them, chrome all over the place. But they still were not brand new; they were old trucks.

I looked at him and said, "This is a brand new truck. This is a 2007. They put it into a cab over model because there's more room underneath for an engine and an electric motor."

The guy said, "Wow, that is so cool." He stood there and was looking all around my truck.

He said, "Wow, I didn't know they'd come so far with all this."

The guys behind him were looking at me like, *"We can see it, you're so full of crap."* I kind of smiled at them.

The guy looks at me and said, "Well, I appreciate your time. I'll let you get going."

I said, "Yeah, I'm just grabbing a little fuel."

"Oh, okay" he said, "well, have a nice day."

They turned around and started walking away, and I could see them all talking to each other. They got maybe thirty or forty feet from me, and the guy who was asking me all the questions turned around and said, "These guys say you're pulling my leg."

I looked over at him and said, "No, this is a hybrid truck."

He turned around and said to his buddies, "I told you so, that's why they put it in a cab over truck."

I just smiled at the other guys when he turned back around and they all took off walking.

I bet that guy ran around and talked to every truck driver he ever saw, telling them he saw the first hybrid truck, and it was a cab over!

There were many different moments with that company; it was quite the adventure.

BETTER LUCKY THAN GOOD

I was out in Pennsylvania driving for a company I don't work for anymore. I'd just delivered a load, and let's just say...I was out of hours.

Back in those days, we used paper logbooks, and as old-time truckers will tell ya, you always had a couple going at the same time.

So, I'd just delivered this load, I was pretty tired, and the company called me up and said, "Hey, we have a load that needs to get down to the other side of Washington DC by morning. Think you can take it down there?"

I said, "Listen, I have *no* hours. I am completely *out*. No matter how I try to make it look on the books, I don't have the hours."

They said, "We'll pay you this much more."

It was a good amount. The load was right there. So, I hooked it.

Still, I had no idea how I was going to make the run look legal.

My "other" logbook showed me in a completely different spot, and my current logbook was shot for hours. There was just no way to make it look good.

"You know what, forget it. I'm just going."

So, I put her in gear and took off.

Later, I got a call from a buddy of mine. He was farther south, coming across Mississippi. I told him what I was doing, then told him about the scale I'd run into just before DC.

He was in the same boat with the scale he had coming up. "I'm driving through. It'll be late early morning by the time I get there. I'm bett'n it'll be closed."

I'd hit mine in the early morning too, but my map suggested there was an alternate route for me. "I'm gonna see if I can run behind mine."

We hung up and I examine the map further, following the back-road parallel to the highway, and behind the scale. I'd just run that, get past the scale, then jump back over onto the highway right above Washington.

My exit came up, I jumped off and hit this little side road.

On the map, the road wasn't marked as illegal for trucks, but every mile or two there were signs saying NO TRUCKS, NO TRAILERS.

I just thought, *"Whatever"* and kept my eye on the map, trying to gauge how soon I could get back on the highway.

Five or six miles later I saw the road leading back to the

highway and took it. The on ramp came into view, I jumped on, and at the end of it was the scale...and the Scale Master standing outside looking directly at me.

I pulled down to the scale where the guy was standing, rolled my window down, I asked, "What's up?"

He shined a flashlight up into my truck. "Uh, you got any passengers in there or anything?"

"No, no, nobody in here whatsoever. Have a good day," I started taking off.

"Whoa, whoa, whoa, whoa, wait a minute."

I stopped, again.

He walked up to my window. "Where you think you're going?"

I told him I thought he was just looking to see if I was carrying passengers.

"No, no." Then he said, "Give me your logbook."

I reached up in my little cubby hole above me and grabbed the logbook—having no idea which one I was grabbing—and handed it to him.

He opened it up and I started explaining, "See, the company called me and wanted me to haul this load last minute. It's a real big hurry. I didn't fill out my logbook when I left. I'm sorry. If you want, I can pull over here and get everything current for you."

"Oh no, no, no, that's all right." He was flipping back through the pages looking at the day before and the day before that.

There was no way this was going to end good.

I asked him again, "Do you want me to pull over and update it? Then you can check it all out?"

He shook his head and handed back my logbook. "I'll have a bunch of trucks coming through here in a little bit and I don't need you tying up room updating your logbook. And, you're just going right down the road?"

"Yeah, I gotta be in there by 5:30." It was probably 4 a.m. at this point.

He told me, again, to get my log all updated when I got there. I promised, again, that I would and pulled out. I got maybe 10 feet when I heard him yelling, "Whoa, Whoa, stop, stop!"

Once again, I stopped and he came walking back to my window. "Let me see that logbook again."

I had thrown the logbook in the top cubbyhole next to the other one and when I handed the logbook to him again, I realized I handed him the "other" logbook.

Oh geez, I'm going to jail.

He opened the logbook, flipped through the pages, and said, "That's what the problem is." He flipped through a couple of pages. "That's what it is."

I finally asked, "What's that?"

"Well I was confused with the time zones, here."

"Yeah, the company is out of Arizona, but I'm out of Wisconsin. So, I run off of the mountain time zone."

He continued flipping pages as if I'd said nothing. "Oh, that's what was confusing me. Okay, you're all good." He handed me my logbook, told me to have a good day, and walked away.

I put her into gear and took off as fast as legally possible.

Back on the highway I called my buddy, "Dude, you'll never guess what just happened to me." I ran through it quick, telling him the story.

He said, "Well you suck, 'cause I got to this scale over here and was tied up about a half an hour explaining my log. Then they hit me with a fine, and shut me down for 10 hours"

I just laughed and said, "Dude, need to learn how to talk less."

Lefty Gomez was right. *'I'd rather be lucky than good.'*

LAST WORDS

You see a lot of different things out on the road. Some really exciting things, lots of boring things, and some crazy things.

Then there are those rare moments where something happens that sticks with you for the rest of your life. This is one of them for me.

I'd been driving for almost two years. I was out in California loading for Illinois. From there I was heading home. I'd been out for quite a while and was ready for some time off.

When I crossed into Nebraska, I was running hard. It was late at night. The highway was mostly vacant, not much around. And then, on the other side of the highway, I saw this car kinda starting to veer from the right lane into the left, then hit the metal wire median. I didn't see any brake lights. I just saw the car go into median, then begin to flip and roll.

My heart sank. I knew it was going to be bad.

I came to a stop on the left lane shoulder, threw my flashers on, struck some flares to let other people know there was a problem —in those days we used flares, now we use mostly triangles— and headed for the car. It was in the middle of the highway on my side. Upside down, steam was coming out all around it.

I looked inside, afraid of what I might see, but there was nobody in the car.

So, I started looking around in the pitch dark. I had no flashlight with me, couldn't see anything. So I walked back and grabbed one of the flares to use as a light and started looking around again.

About 50 to 70 feet away from the car I found a young lady laying in a ditch. She was moaning a little bit. I tried to talk to her, tried to see what was going on and how I could help her. But she was not very responsive. I had a hoodie on, and she was bleeding pretty badly from her head.

So I took off my hoodie and gently wrapped it around her, kind of bunched it underneath her head. Then I took off running back to my truck for my cell phone. I had a small service carrier and was out in Nebraska. I had no coverage, no signal. It was, you know, a different time. Cell phones weren't like they are today.

But I had this little computer thing in my truck. Not like the new ELDs (electronic logging device) in the trucks now, but I could send a message to dispatch. I told them where I was, about the young lady I found, that she was losing a lot of blood, told them to call the police, and get an ambulance out here ASAP. I sent the message off, and I ran back to her. I could see the woman--really she was a girl--kinda trying to move, her arms flailing.

As I came up to her again, she saw me, and I think I kind of frightened her a little bit. I tried to explain to her that I found her, that I'd messaged somebody to get help, and she should probably lay still.

She laid there for a couple of minutes crying and I started talking to her, asking her about her arm which was obviously broken. There was a bone sticking out of it.

She said she couldn't feel her right leg at all.

I tried to assess her a little bit. You could see bruising everywhere on her. But every time I tried to move her a little bit she'd cry out in pain. So, I just sat down next to her, held her hand and started talking to her.

We talked about different things and it seemed to be helping her. She was calming down a little.

But every once in awhile, she would start to glaze over, lose consciousness a little bit.

I had a bottle of water that I'd brought back from the truck and I kept splashing little sprinkles in her face to keep her awake. I tried to get her to drink some, too, but she didn't want any.

Keeping her awake seemed the best option, so I kept talking to her. She cried some talking about her parents and this road trip she was on, and how she was thinking about moving.

She also talked about the things that she was sorry for in her life.

I could see her changing, her coloring, her demeanor. She was getting worse. So I said, "I'm going to run back to my truck and check the message, make sure it's gone through and see if they replied."

She didn't want me to leave, but I really wanted to make sure that help was coming. So I ran back to my truck, punched up the computer, and sure enough, I'd gotten a confirmation from dispatch.

When I got back to her, she was crying again, and I told her that the message had gone through, and help was on the way.

Then I saw a car coming. It pulled over and I yelled for the driver. It was a woman. She came over and sat with the girl, too. I told her help was coming then asked her if she had a phone. She didn't. She was also kind of looking the girl over and then we looked at each other. We knew it wasn't going to end well.

So we just sat there holding her hand trying to keep her calm and lucid.

Then the woman asked the girl, "do you know God?"

The girl looked at her and said, "yes, I do. Because I grew up in a Christian home. I hate to say it, but I've parted ways from God. I haven't been very good, you know, I've sinned a lot."

The woman looked at her and told her, "He will forgive if you ask."

And we sat out there with this girl, in a ditch, holding hands, and prayed together, as the girl asked forgiveness.

When she got done, she looked at me, and I could tell she had a peace about her. She just…she was very calm.

Then she thanked me for stopping and being nice.

I told her, "of course. It's the right thing to do, you know."

Then she said, "I think my time is here." She said it so calmly. It was…it was amazing. "My wallet should be in my purse. I don't know where it is, but if you find it, you will find my address and my name. Could you please contact my parents and tell them that I asked forgiveness and I think God heard me. Tell my parents that I love them, and I will see them again.

I told her I would take care of that, but she just needed to hang on and she'd be okay.

She grabbed my arm with her other hand and said, "it *is* okay" and I could see the life drain from her.

The woman that had stopped to help started crying, and I started to cry, and I sat there, holding her as she passed away.

A few minutes later a man and another woman, who was a nurse, came over. She checked the girl's pulse, asked us a few questions, then agreed she was gone. There was nothing more that could be done.

Finally, we heard sirens.

The police arrived with the ambulance that came right down to where we were. By now the girl had been gone about 30 minutes.

When the paramedics were done asking me questions, I got up, collected myself the best I possibly could and walked over to the police officer. I said, "we need to find her purse."

He assured me they'd find it.

I said, "I need to find it. The last thing she asked me to do was find her purse. It will have her address in it. She wanted me to contact her parents and give them a message."

The Police officer was really nice about it. He could have told me to get lost, but he let me hang out there. We searched the area and I gave my statement about everything that happened.

When we found her purse with her wallet, the police officer said, "I'm not really supposed to do this. But what I'm going to do is try and get ahold of her parents and I'm going to give her parents your name and everything and ask them if they want to speak with you."

I said, "that's fine. But could you please tell them that she gave me a message that she wants me to tell them?"

"Well, just give me the message and I'll pass it along."

I said, "I don't want to do that. I don't want this passed along and messed up or to come from somebody who wasn't there with her."

He said he understood.

So, I went back to the truck and I cried for quite a while, tried to gather myself. It was hard.

I'd never had a death in my family or a death close to me. So, it was hard to go through that. Death happens to everyone. It was just very, very difficult being there, talking with her, getting to know her through the conversations we had and then have that happen.

A couple of days later I got a phone call. It was her parents. I talked to them and they asked me what happened, how was she, and I really wanted to kind of sugar coat it a little bit, that she wasn't in pain. But I didn't want there to be any deception. I felt like they really needed to know exactly what happened

So, I walked them through the whole thing, and I told them that I don't think she felt much of the pain because she was mostly in shock and that she went very peacefully.

Then I gave her parents the message she asked me to pass along.

There was a long silence before they spoke again.

Then they said that their heart was broken because they lost their daughter, but now their heart was also joyous because they knew she asked forgiveness for her sins and she went in a very peaceful way and they would see her again.

I have since spoken to these parents probably 15 to 20 times. We've actually become very close, and we usually speak about once a year.

I don't think it's because they're holding onto the memory of their daughter. They're very much at peace about it. I think it's that they loved their daughter very much and I was there at the end. We have a connection.

For the first few years they'd always call me around that time and we'd just talk. Every once in a while, their daughter would come up and they'd tell me stories about her.

Now we're just close friends.

Since then, a very good friend of mine died. I went to his funeral. I thought I was fine, but as soon as I saw him, it brought back the memories.

Like I said, I do understand death happens. I just thought she was very special, and it took a while for me to understand, to comprehend, why it had to happen.

There are reasons for everything.

But we must move on and keep putting one foot in front of the other.

That is one of the reasons why, at the end of my videos, I often say "If you're not having a good day today, you can always try again tomorrow."

His mercies are new every morning.

The End

ACKNOWLEDGMENTS

I want to thank Brian and Nina Paules at *ePublishing Works!* along with their daughter Anna. Without their tireless effort, this book would not exist. They made it easy; all I had to do was talk to my windshield!

I also want to thank John at JBG Travels. John spent nearly a year trying to get me to start a YouTube channel, and without the YouTube channel, this book wouldn't exist.

ABOUT THE AUTHOR

Veteran trucker, Long-Haul Larry hails from the eastern lowlands of Wisconsin, north of Milwaukee, but can be found anywhere along America's vast highways piloting Big Blue along with Chicken Johnny.

Larry firmly believes, "If you're gonna drive 'em, you better be able to fix 'em." Using his natural mechanical aptitude and experience as a truck mechanic, he keeps Big Blue "running the miles" and their deliveries on time.

Join Larry and Chicken Johnny in their daily adventures on the Long-Haul Larry YouTube Channel at the link shown below.

What's up with the chicken, you ask? You'll have to look for Chicken Johnny on Larry's YouTube channel to find out.

www.TRUCKEROLOGY.com

 youtube.com/intermodaltrucker

thanks for the support

Thanks for the Support

CPSIA information can be obtained
at www.ICGtesting.com
Printed in the USA
BVHW042337140420
577619BV00001B/3

2 370000 753410